Photographers: Aquarium Products; Dr. Herbert R. Axelrod; Dr. Warren E. Burgess; Cole Enterprises; J. Elias; Estes, Clifford W. Co. Inc.; courtesy FTFFA; S. Frank; Frickhinger; Michael Gilroy; Dr. Harry Grier; Rolf C. Hagen (USA) Corp.; H. Hansen; T.J. Horeman; Dr. D. Jacobs; Rene Jez; Rodney Jonklaas; Jaroslav Kadlec; Burkhard Kahl; Dr. Karl Knaack; U. Korber; Kremser; Vachau Lahoda; Horst Linke; Marine Enterprise; Midori Shobo; F. Mohlmann; Aaron Norman; O'Dell Industries Inc.; J. Palicka; Klaus Paysan; Perfecto Manufacturing Inc.; Python Products; Quitschau; Hans Joachim Richter; Mervin F. Roberts; Andre Roth; G.E. Schmida; Andreas Spreinat; Heinrich Stolz; Edward C. Taylor; D. Terver; Deiter Untergasser; Jörg Vierke; Wardley Products; Ruda Zukal. **Artists:** Lisa Marie O'Connell; John R. Quinn.

Title page: Axelrod's rainbowfish (*Melanotaenia herbertaxelrodi*).

1995 Edition

Distributed in the UNITED STATES to the Pet Trade by T.F.H. Publications, Inc., One T.F.H. Plaza, Neptune City, NJ 07753; distributed in the UNITED STATES to the Bookstore and Library Trade by National Book Network, Inc. 4720 Boston Way, Lanham MD 20706; in CANADA to the Pet Trade by H & L Pet Supplies Inc., 27 Kingston Crescent, Kitchener, Ontario N2B 2T6; Rolf C. Hagen Ltd., 3225 Sartelon Street, Montreal 382 Quebec; in CANADA to the Book Trade by Vanwell Publishing Ltd., 1 Northrup Crescent, St. Catharines, Ontario L2M 6P5 ; in ENGLAND by T.F.H. Publications, PO Box 15, Waterlooville PO7 6BQ; in AUSTRALIA AND THE SOUTH PACIFIC by T.F.H. (Australia), Pty. Ltd., Box 149, Brookvale 2100 N.S.W., Australia; in NEW ZEALAND by Brooklands Aquarium Ltd. 5 McGiven Drive, New Plymouth, RD1 New Zealand; in Japan by T.F.H. Publications, Japan—Jiro Tsuda, 10-12-3 Ohjidai, Sakura, Chiba 285, Japan; in SOUTH AFRICA by Lopis (Pty) Ltd., P.O. Box 39127, Booysens, 2016, Johannesburg, South Africa. Published by T.F.H. Publications, Inc. Printed in Spain.

YOUR HOME AQUARIUM

JÖRG VIERKE
Translated by U. Erich Friese

The kissing gourami (*Helostoma temmincki*) is popular with many home aquarists. This fish, however, gets large and quite aggressive as it grows older; therefore, it is not an ideal community tank inhabitant.

CONTENTS

Introduction

**Rosy tetra
(*Hyphessobrycon
bentosi*).**

*"Following this
guide will enable
anyone to
establish a
beautiful and
fascinating
community tank
for long-lasting
viewing
pleasure."*

Working with exotic fish and water plants is among the most fascinating hobbies one can have. Yet a novice attempting to venture into aquarium keeping without any prior knowledge can quickly come to grief. Many fish tanks now collecting dust in attics or basements are evidence of such failures. The sad part about this is that in most cases a few words of constructive advice could have helped those who gave up in despair.

This book will attempt to give reliable help to the novice, the beginning aquarist. It will convey all necessary information needed for setting up and then successfully maintaining an aquarium and its inhabitants.

There are many ways of setting up a home aquarium, decorating it attractively and selecting colorful, interesting fish. But for the novice, setting up an aquarium and then selecting suitable fish can be a bit of a gamble. In the following text I would like to present a plan for setting up a tank which is not only easy to follow but also leads to an attractive home aquarium. Following this guide will enable anyone to establish a beautiful and fascinating community tank for long-lasting viewing pleasure.

Young hobbyists often do not have the money to set up a large community tank. For them I have described an alternative in the form of a miniature aquarium, which even affords the opportunity of fish breeding. With this I do hope that many aquarists will realize the deep insights into biological interactions that are provided here and the profound satisfaction that this hobby can bring.

In addition, I also hope that this book will become a reliable guide for your involvement with aquarium fish. I am convinced that you will soon agree: aquarium keeping is a fascinating hobby and a continuous source of new discoveries!

Why Exotic Fish?

Tiger barb (*Capoeta tetrazona*). One of the joys of keeping tropical fish is learning about the habits and personalities of various species.

Maybe you saw a magnificently decorated aquarium at a friend's home, or maybe you were fortunate enough to observe some fish parents tenderly caring for their young; this easily creates the desire for your own aquarium. Simply by observing a few important points, and without having to invest much money, an attractive community aquarium can be set up with graceful underwater plants and some colorful, interesting fishes; this is, of course, apart from the inevitable initial equipment and accessory costs. The recurrent costs of keeping are certainly much lower than the expenses commonly incurred for most other pets. Even things like holidays and extended vacations do not pose any problems.

There are indeed few other opportunities to observe and learn about biological interactions so graphically and clearly as during the process of setting up and caring for an aquarium and its inhabitants. An aquarium is not merely a collection of plants and animals, but instead it is a closed, fully functional biological community. As with any other living system, an aquarium must not be constantly interfered with, such as through attempts to "improve" matters by too frequent cleaning and re-arranging things. Observation and restraint are the main operative words for the most effective aquarium care. This approach certainly conforms to our appreciation of nature and its ways. Maybe this is the very reason for the popularity of keeping aquariums.

"There are indeed few other opportunities to observe and learn about biological interactions so graphically and clearly as during the process of setting up and caring for an aquarium and its inhabitants."

The Correct Aquarium

A school of red rainbowfish (*Glossolepis incisus*).

"Beginning aquarists are often under the (seriously mistaken) impression that it is easier to start out with a small tank than with a large one. Nothing can be further from the truth."

Aquariums are available in a variety of designs and sizes. The decision for a particular tank depends solely upon individual esthetic taste, funds available and space available in a home. Virtually all commercially available aquariums fulfill their intended purposes. Today there is essentially one major type of aquarium tank available at pet shops and tropical fish specialty stores, the all-glass aquarium, one in which the sides and bottom of the tank are held

Center and bottom: Your local aquarium dealer will have a large selection of tanks from which to choose. Many modern tanks are made of glass panes that are bonded together with silicone rubber cement; others are constructed of molded acrylic material.

together as a unit by silicone rubber cement. The disadvantage of plastic aquariums is the fact that they are more prone to becoming scratched than glass tanks. This is particularly critical when cleaning the inside of plastic tanks; tiny grains of sand can act like "glass cutters" and cause unsightly scratching.

Beginning aquarists are often under the (seriously mistaken) impression that it is easier to start out with a small tank than with a large one. Nothing can be further from the truth. The larger the tank, the easier it is to maintain a stable water quality. Moreover, the more space available for the fish, the better they can grow and develop to maturity. On the other hand, very small tanks often require more intense monitoring (and greater aquaristic experience) than larger tanks.

The ideal tank for a beginner should have a volume of about 20 gallons. The examples given in this book about setting up and specific maintenance refer to such a "standard aquarium." But at the same time, these examples can be adjusted for even larger tanks.

HEATING AND LIGHTING

An aquarium without artificial light is unthinkable. Tropical water plants require 12 to 14 hours of light daily throughout the entire year. During the winter months we would not have enough light for these water plants, and during summer months there would be an excess

of light. This would cause excessive algae growth. It is advisable to purchase an aquarium cover with built-in fluorescent light(s) at the same time the tank is bought. Your dealer will be able to advise you about the proper wattage of the bulbs. Caring for tropical fish and plants is very much simpler than for native species. However, we also need an aquarium

Above: Aquarium heaters come in different wattages to suit tanks of different sizes. The heaters shown here, for example, range from 50 to 300 watts. Photo courtesy of Hagen.

Center: Aquaria can be specifically designed to complement your home decor. *Far left:* Generally an aquarium kit containing all the essentials can be obtained at a cost lower than the total cost of all of the individual items in the kit. Some kits contain the tank as well as all of the other equipment. Photo courtesy of California Aquarium Supply Co.

Consult your local dealer for recommendations about fluorescent bulbs of suitable wattage and color spectrum for your particular aquarium. Photo courtesy of Hagen.

"An aquarium filter has the task of removing turbidity-causing suspended particles from the water."

Test kits that enable the hobbyist to monitor various factors affecting the quality of aquarium water, such as its pH and hardness and ammonia/ nitrate levels, are available at pet shops and tropical fish specialty stores. Photo courtesy of Aquarium Pharmaceuticals, Inc.

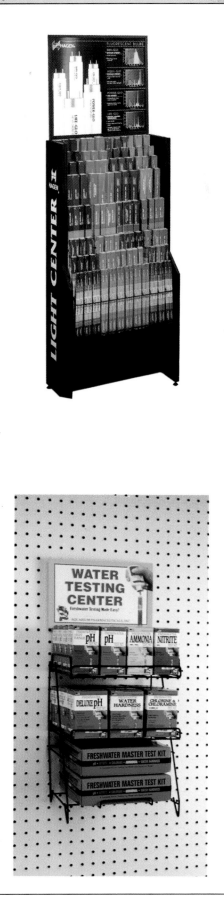

heater, because room temperatures would be insufficient for our animals in the long run. In most cases it is best to buy a combined heater/thermostat unit, a so-called automatically regulated heater (automatic heater). Combined heater/thermostat units are available in both submergible and non-submergible form; the advantage of the submergible heater is that it can be concealed from view more easily.

THE FILTER

The acquisition of a filter is highly recommended. An aquarium filter has the task of removing turbidity-causing suspended particles from the water. The aquarium plants are particularly grateful for this and, of course, it improves the esthetic appearance of the tank quite substantially. Moreover, the water movement caused by the filter is of importance to the fish. Most species are adapted by nature to water currents of some sort. Additionally, the filter current prevents undesirable temperature gradients in the tank water. It also expedites gas exchange between water and the air above. Consequently, our fish will not suffer respiratory difficulties.

An airstone operated by air supplied from an air pump would also inhibit temperature gradients in the tank and expedite gas exchange. However, airstones are less effective than filters and, because they are very effective in expelling carbon dioxide from the water, detract from optimal plant growth.

The choice of available filters is diverse. It is beyond the scope of this book to list the advantages and disadvantages of each individual type of filter. A small

equipment that can be very valuable is an automatic water changer, which performs the highly important function of making frequent partial changes of water without any effort by the hobbyist and without any chance of being forgotten by the hobbyist.

inside filter operated by a quiet vibrator pump is ideally suited for a small community tank, and larger tanks can use power filters (either hanging type or canister type) or undergravel filters or any of the other types recommended by your dealer.

USEFUL ACCESSORIES

Apart from standard aquarium equipment, the trade offers a multitude of other gadgets. There are only a few things we still need: a thermometer for monitoring the water temperature, and a fish net to catch and remove fish from the tank. Also possibly required are a glass cleaner and a water hose for siphoning off water and debris off the bottom, plus test kits for testing the quality of the water. Another piece of

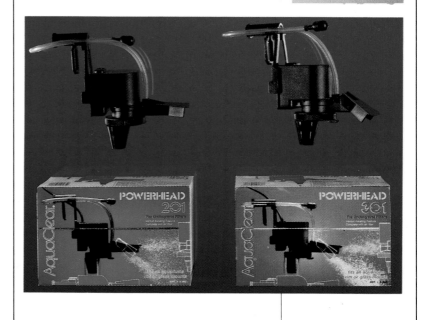

Aeration in the aquarium is of greater importance to some fish species than to others. Because a number of popular aquarium species (like the male *Betta splendens* shown here, for example) can breathe atmospheric oxygen to a certain extent they are less dependent than most other species on the oxygen content of the water. Photo by K.Tanaka.

Artist's rendering of the placement and camouflage of an underground filter.

Setting Up the Tank

An aquarium is not only supposed to be esthetically pleasing but it must also be suitable for its inhabitants. Fortunately these two ideas are quite compatible, because whatever suits our fish also appeals to our sense of beauty. Fish need ample room for swimming, but they must also have a few plant thickets for cover where they can also hide, if need be. In such a confined space—even with large aquariums, when compared against the large bodies of water in the wild—there can be arguments among some of the inhabitants. Therefore, it is important that a weaker or smaller fish can easily find protection in thick plant cover. Similar protection is also afforded by large rocks or suspended aerial roots from terrestrial plants. Consequently, these items are more than just decoration.

WHERE TO PLACE THE TANK

I want an aquarium, but where do I put it? The answer to this question depends very much on the respective home situation. One place that must be avoided is a window sill!! There are two reasons for this. Firstly, fish do not look very good against back lighting, which is essentially unavoidable when an aquarium is placed in front of a window. Secondly—and more importantly—an aquarium close

Your home aquarium can be as simple or as elaborate as you like once the basic requirements are met.

"An aquarium is not only supposed to be esthetically pleasing but it must also be suitable for its inhabitants. Fortunately these two ideas are quite compatible, because whatever suits our fish also appeals to our sense of beauty."

Make sure that whatever stand you use to hold your aquarium tank is more than sturdy enough for the weight.

When placing your tank on the stand, it is a good idea to place a piece of styrofoam or similar material underneath; this will help reduce stress on the glass and will help the tank lie evenly.

"We want to position our aquarium in such a way that we can easily watch the fish in the best of comfort. Therefore, it should be at eye level when the viewer is sitting down."

to the window would get too much light and the inevitable algae plague would be very difficult to avoid. The best location would be the darkest spot in a room! The artificial illumination, which we must have anyway, makes us independent of daylight. The less daylight we get into our aquarium the better off we are! In addition, an illuminated aquarium impresses the viewer more when it is in a dark location.

Wherever we end up placing the aquarium—be it on a desk or on a special stand along a wall—we must always remember to be within easy reach of electrical outlets and remember that the tank must be serviced (inside and outside) without difficulty. The latter is important for occasional tank maintenance. Placing the tank on a shelf can make service access extremely difficult, even dangerous. Moreover, serious consideration must be given to the anticipated weight of an aquarium full of water, rocks, etc., when placed on a shelf. A 100-liter (25 gallon) tank full of water weighs 100 kg (220 pounds) plus its own (empty) weight, and this does not include sand and rocks! With such a weight a sturdy table would make a far better and safer support for an aquarium.

Now a final point. We want to position our aquarium in such a way that we can easily watch the fish in the best of comfort. Therefore, it should be at eye level when the viewer is sitting down. Many aquarists tend to overlook this when placing and setting up a tank.

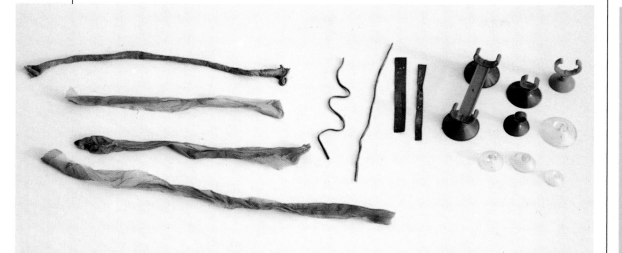

There are several types of anchors made specifically for aquarium plants. These devices hold the plants in place; they are especially helpful for the first-time planter.

MATERIALS

The basic materials needed are sand or gravel, a few rocks, and decorative roots. The water plants to be used are discussed separately.

Sand or gravel is required as substrate for the plants. Some careful consideration should go into the selection and preparation of the substrate. If mistakes are avoided the substrate can remain in the tank for years. Garden soil and fertilized flowerpot soil must be avoided. Beach sand, because of its high carbonate components, is also highly unsatisfactory. Pure sand and gravel have proven to be the best substances. Personally, I prefer fine-grained gravel (grain size 1 to 5 mm)

"Sand or gravel is required as substrate for the plants. Some careful consideration should go into the selection and preparation of the substrate."

Artificial decorations can add interest and a touch of color to an aquarium, and they can provide welcome refuge for species that feel more secure in nooks and caves. Photo courtesy of Blue Ribbon Pet Products.

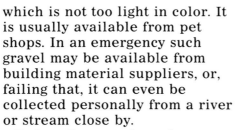

which is not too light in color. It is usually available from pet shops. In an emergency such gravel may be available from building material suppliers, or, failing that, it can even be collected personally from a river or stream close by.

Before the gravel can be introduced into the tank it must be thoroughly washed in order to remove any organic material or clay particles. The gravel is washed, stirring it continuously as water is run through the washing container (a bucket), until the water above the gravel

remains clear. Even though this is sometimes a somewhat laborious task, thoroughness is important. Every aquarist soon develops his or her own methods. One may use his hand to stir up the gravel while another may prefer a wooden spoon. Some aquarists prefer the method of sifting the gravel under running water. With some degree of thoroughness it may take a quarter of an hour or more until the gravel is clean; that is, there are no more gray "clouds" rising from the gravel in the bucket when it is stirred up under water, but only some very fine sand

fish. Experience has shown that in newly established aquariums there is never any danger of a lack of nutrition for water plants, but there is always the risk of over-fertilization. Moreover, a large supply of plant nutrients always tends to favor the development of algae during this early stage. Then the substrate, including rocks and plants, will start to be covered with a green, musty-smelling layer of algae within a few days after such a tank has been set up.

Rocks most suitable for an

grains which will settle again quickly.

It is particularly easy to wash the sand outdoors. There we can fill the wash bucket halfway with sand or gravel and use a running garden hose to flush and stir the sand simultaneously until it is completely clean.

Even advanced aquarists sometimes still believe that this washed bottom substrate must be fertilized; after all, nothing can grow on nothing! Nevertheless, such initial fertilization must be omitted. During the early stage our plants are quite capable of removing sufficient nutrients from the aquarium water. Soon there will be ample fertilizer in the water from the excretion of

Artist's rendering of a recently planted tank. Note the asymmetrical layout.

"Even advanced aquarists sometimes believe that this washed bottom substrate must be fertilized; after all, nothing can grow on nothing! Nevertheless, such initial fertilization must be omitted."

Artist's rendering of a sprig of water sprite (*Ceratopteris thalicroides sumatra*).

A stunning coffee table aquarium from Coles.

"A realistic underwater atmosphere can easily be created by the introduction of a bizarre-shaped tree root."

***Vallisneria gigantea.** This species is also known as the giant val.*

to estimate the right size needed. Experience has shown that most aquarists tend to select pieces of wood that are too large! In order to avoid any problems with these roots (flotation, fungus development, etc.) the wood must first be soaked in water. Inevitably, this will take at least several days (sometimes even weeks, depending on the type of wood) until enough water has been absorbed so that the root will no longer float and instead will sink to the bottom. This process can, however, be hastened by boiling the root in a large cooking pot. This forces the air out of the wood pores and the root can no longer float.

aquarium are those of a crystalline type, such as granite; slate is also very useful. I must warn against the use of carbonate rocks, because they can cause an undesired increase in water hardness. If in doubt, a quick hydrochloric (muriatic) acid test can be made. A few drops of the acid are placed on the rock to be tested. If "bubbling" (foam) develops it contains calcium, and it should not be used in the aquarium. If we are alert during this early stage, when adding substrate and rocks, not to introduce any calcareous substances into the tank, we must then not make the mistake of using clam and snail shells as decorative aquarium items. All seashells are virtually pure calcium!

A realistic underwater atmosphere can easily be created by the introduction of a bizarre-shaped tree root. Rarely are aquarists lucky enough to find suitable, well-leached roots in some pond, swamp or similar habitat, but specialist aquarium shops usually have a wide selection of bog roots and driftwood for sale. It is important

PLANTS

I cannot imagine a nicely decorated community tank without plants. Of course, there are exceptions such as a marine tank or those specially set up for herbivorous (plant-eating) fishes, but these are not considered here.

Water plants are far more than just aquarium decorations. They

also serve to provide hiding places for the fish, a task which is also fulfilled by rocks and tree roots. The water plants in an aquarium serve mainly to inhibit the development of blue-green algae. This type of algae is a simple-structured, microscopically small plant which can be recognized as such only under high magnification. Under certain conditions blue-green algae can occur in such massive proportions that they coat the entire interior of an aquarium with an ugly bright green or brownish layer. (In spite of the name blue-green, these algae are never blue.) These algae "explosions" are the reason why many a beginning aquarist gave up the hobby.

There is a sure-fire preventive against this sort of blue-green algae development. In fact, every aquarium has small amounts of this kind of algae, but ample planting with water plants—the

"higher" plants, i.e. the actual aquarium plants—contributes quite substantially to keeping algae development in check. Higher water plants and algae, specifically blue-green algae, are actually competitors. Where there are higher plants growing, algae find it difficult to maintain themselves. On the other hand, once algae have taken over, aquarium plants can usually no longer compete and begin to decline. When we take this sort of competition between these two plant groups into consideration

Top and center: Artist's rendering of part of the planting process.

"Under certain conditions blue-green algae can occur in such massive proportions that they coat the entire interior of an aquarium with an ugly bright green or brownish layer."

Far left: Products designed to provide a stable medium in which rooted plants can establish themselves and grow are widely available. Photo courtesy of Aquarium Products.

and so establish an environment which favors the higher plants, algae will hardly ever become a problem.

Therefore, it is particularly important to introduce as many plants as possible when the aquarium is first set up. The more higher plants there are in the aquarium, the better! To start out, select plants which grow particularly fast. This sort of plant has a high nutrient intake, so that there is little nutrient material left for algal growth. These plants have the added advantage that they are relatively cheap. After a few weeks, when the aquarium has become properly "established," some of these rapidly growing plants can be replaced with more demanding and decorative species.

Among water plants, one distinguishes between those which are rooted in the substrate and the so-called floating plants. The latter are not always desired in an aquarium because they have a tendency to reduce the amount of light badly needed by the plants growing in the substrate below. Nevertheless, some floating plants are indeed quite attractive. Moreover, many fish like floating plants because of the protective cover they afford. After all, fishes out in open water would indeed be far safer under a floating plant cover than in an area where the water surface is wide open. In fact, some fish build their nests among floating plants and young fish find ample protection and hiding places among them.

Especially recommended are the various floating water sprites, *Ceratopteris* species. All have large leaves and decorative, fringed (suspended) root stocks. As tender as their leaves may look, they are in no danger of being gnawed on by fish or snails. These ferns reproduce completely without our help by means of daughter plants which sprout off the leaves of the parent plant. Still, they do not reproduce to such an extent that they become a burden. Nevertheless, even *Ceratopteris* should be pruned regularly, even though we may regret having to dispose of such sturdy plants. In the interest of the rooted plants along the bottom this simply has to be done.

The aquarium plants actively growing on the bottom can be placed into two categories: stemmed plants and bottom dwellers. Stemmed plants have leaves that come off a stem which usually grows upward. On the other hand, bottom dwellers do not have a stem. Their leaves originate, rosette-like, from the same central location. When planting the bottom dwellers we have to make sure that the leaf "heart" is not covered by sand or gravel. To be on the safe side the plants should be inserted into the substrate so that the upper root bases are still

Cryptocoryne willisii. **This species reaches a maximum size of 10 to 12 cm.**

just barely visible above the bottom. Once a plant has been covered in excess by sand and gravel it has little or no chance to force its delicate leaves through and above the substrate.

Of course, this problem does not exist with stemmed plants. A stem which has lost its lower leaves can readily be trimmed back and then replanted. No special care has to be taken about the roots. In fact, it is advisable to cut a large portion of the roots off because they are no longer of any use to the plant. Most will die and the plants will grow new roots. Those old roots would only cause patches of decay in the substrate. Incidentally, this can of course also happen with bottom dwelling plants. Here too part of the root system should be cut off.

"To be on the safe side the plants should be inserted into the substrate so that the upper root bases are still just barely visible above the bottom."

Java fern (*Microsorium pteropus***). Attach this plant to a rock or piece of driftwood— Java fern should not be planted in the gravel.**

Generally it is advisable to trim all roots back to about half of their original length, except in very short plants. Here we would forego any root removal; otherwise it is often difficult to secure short plants in the substrate.

There are also profound differences in the reproduction between these two types of plants. It is a rare case indeed if an aquarist is so lucky as to actually obtain seeds from his aquarium plants. Usually water plant reproduction under aquarium conditions is by means of "runners" among the bottom dwelling plants. In plants which reproduce through sprouting shoots, these are pinched off. This is a very easy procedure.

Each newly planted shoot will develop into a new plant, provided there is sufficient light. If the mother plant remains in the substrate it will produce another shoot within a few days or weeks.

Ludwigia peruviana. **Plants of this genus require generous amounts of light in the aquarium.**

"It is a rare case indeed if an aquarist is so lucky as to actually obtain seeds from his aquarium plants."

Left: **A lotus (***Nymphaea rubra devoniensis***).** *Right:* **Dwarf Amazon swordplant (***Echinodorus tenellus***).**

The development of "runners" in bottom dwellers is rarely ever that fast; in fact, in some species it may never happen. In other species, runners extending far into the open water have to be pressed into the substrate and weighted down with a rock so that the adventitious plant can become established. Other bottom dwellers produce runners which extend underneath the surface of the sand or gravel layer. This is the reason why a new plant sometimes emerges some distance away from a

parent plant. *Vallisneria* and *Cryptocoryne* are masters of this type of reproduction. Be careful *not* to separate the young plant too early. Usually it is not even necessary or sensible to cut off such runners.

HOW TO SET UP THE TANK

Right at the start the budding aquarist should establish and then always maintain a certain sequential procedure.

Firstly, we must find a suitable location for the aquarium. The relevant points about this topic have already been mentioned. The most important thing to remember is: not too much

daylight for the aquarium!

At this point we must also decide on the fish we wish to keep, because this has a significant bearing on how to set up the tank. The sensible thing, of course, is to select those species which will thrive under the water conditions that we can provide. Here the total hardness of the water is of decisive significance. The total hardness—often just referred to as hardness—indicates the amount of calcium and magnesium salts which are dissolved in the water. Most pet shops in your home town will be able to give you relevant information about this. Otherwise, a telephone call to your local water board or similar authority will get you that information. Your pet shop also sells inexpensive water test kits.

If we have our heart set on a well-planted community tank with lots of colorful fishes, we can only hope that the water is not too hard. Water hardness in excess of 20 degrees (German) total hardness is not acceptable for most tropical fish.

Next we have to test the tank to

"The total hardness—often just referred to as hardness—indicates the amount of calcium and magnesium salts which are dissolved in the water."

Ludwigia repens. Ludwigia species sometimes develop a reddish or purple pigment on their leaves.

Water wisteria (Hygrophila difformis).

23

McCulloch's rainbowfish (*Melanotaenia maccullochii*). This species is also known as the dwarf Australian rainbowfish.

"Can you imagine the reaction of someone looking at your tank if he can see your colorful flower wallpaper through the back glass of your aquarium."

make sure it does not leak. Normally one would assume that a newly purchased aquarium is absolutely watertight, but it can happen that such a tank leaks. Nothing is worse than discovering that a tank which has been set up painstakingly with love and care does leak. Sooner or later even advanced hobbyists will make this sort of unpleasant discovery, so it pays to make this simple test the first step in the actual setting up procedure.

Can you imagine the reaction of someone looking at your tank if he can see your colorful flower wallpaper through the back glass of your aquarium? In order to avoid this it is advisable to place a special aquarium background between the tank and the wall behind it. Pet shops have a variety of such aquarium backgrounds available, and your taste and imagination are really

the only things that matter here. Alternatively, aquarium back glass can also be painted in a variety of realistic or surrealistic patterns. There are no limits here except one's own imagination.

Once the back glass is set up then the tank can be put into its designated position. The tank must be set on a reasonably thick and flexible mat in order to avoid stress and tension to the tank structure, which can lead to leaks or—worse—cracked glass. For that purpose cut out a piece of felt or styrofoam to the correct size (i.e., to fit closely to the bottom of the tank). In an emergency a piece of thick cardboard will also serve the same purpose.

Now it's time to wash the gravel. How this can be done simply and easily was previously discussed. While we are at it, the rocks should be scrubbed briefly with a brush. It is not a disaster when the first gravel layer is not completely clean. On the contrary, the plants will profit from any clay remnants left in the sand or gravel. When we later add the plants, the water will not turn cloudy because the first gravel layer is covered over again by a second, well-washed layer. Therefore, it is important that the substrate is not stirred up again when the tank is filled with water. For that purpose we put a saucer on the bottom of the tank and the water is poured gently into the saucer. The water should be pre-warmed so that it is lukewarm. A hose is the best tool for filling a tank. It should be plastic and have a length of at least 2 meters and a diameter of about 1 cm.

Should the hose be long enough that it reaches all the way to the bathroom or kitchen it can be attached directly to the water tap. The pre-warmed water is then fed directly from the bathroom tap into the tank. Failing that, a water bucket can serve the same purpose. The water does not need to be poured into the tank all at once. Instead, we siphon from the bucket into the tank. In that case, though, the bucket must be placed higher than the aquarium (for proper gravity feed of the water). To start the siphon, one end of the hose is placed below the water in the bucket and suction (by mouth) is applied to the other hose end until the flow almost reaches the mouth. The outflow end is then closed off through pressure applied with a thumb and it is not opened until it is placed inside the tank. If the siphon has been started properly the bucket will empty quickly. No doubt every aquarist will experience sooner or later (mostly sooner!) what it feels like to get a mouth full of water, but this method is still the most effective and aquarists generally cannot do without it. The very same physical principle can also be applied in reverse; that is, water can be siphoned from the tank into a bucket, provided it is located at a level which is below the surface of the aquarium.

Once the aquarium is half-full, the water inflow is stopped and the saucer is removed. Now the time has come to start planting!

By now we have acquired all necessary plants according to our plant scheme and the contemplated planting layout. Here it is important to remember to trim the roots. Also keep in mind that bottom dwellers must not be pushed too deeply into the sand or gravel! Special care must be taken with stemmed plants so that the delicate stems are not crushed when they are pushed into the substrate. Thumb pressure can easily crush the stems, so let us use a better

method! A small planting hole is dug into the substrate just by pushing a finger in. Then the stem is inserted into the hole, which is filled in again from all sides. This is the same method as used with garden plants, but is much easier to use under water.

Are all plants properly secured now on the bottom? Now the aquarium is filled all the way to the top. I have already discussed

"No doubt every aquarist will experience sooner or later (mostly sooner!) what it feels like to get a mouth full of water..."

Myriophyllum verticillatum. **This species is widely distributed throughout Europe and North America.**

Aquarium thermometers come in a number of different types, all handy and relatively inexpensive. The type shown can be attached right to the glass of the tank. Photo courtesy of Hagen.

how this is done without stirring everything up again; therefore, do *not* forget the saucer. Moreover, if possible, use filling water with the correct temperature—that is, the water is already properly mixed in the bucket (or adjusted tap water directly from the bathroom!) so that the final temperature is somewhere between 23° and 28°C (73–82°F). Do *not* make the mistake of trying to correct a low temperature in the tank by adding hot water! This is one of the easiest ways to burst

Aquarium thermometers come in a number of different types, all handy and relatively inexpensive. The type shown can be attached right to the glass of the tank. Photo courtesy of Hagen.

aquarium glass. The ideal situation is to reach the required water temperature just when the tank is full or nearly so.

No matter how meticulous you are when filling the tank, it can happen that individual plants become up-rooted and dislodged. These are retrieved and then simply re-planted. While your hand is still in the water you can then adjust other plants which have been pushed too far into the substrate or are not planted straight.

Now our tank is almost completely set up! If we still want to introduce some floating plants, now is the time. The thermometer, which we have used repeatedly (to check the filling water temperature) is now secured to one wall of the tank. When we purchased the thermometer, presumably we also acquired a suction cup holder at the same time. With this we attach the thermometer to one wall of the aquarium in a position where it does not spoil the esthetic appearance of the tank but still enables us to get accurate temperature readings.

At this stage we also finish installing the filter and start it up. Hopefully we have also been given detailed operating

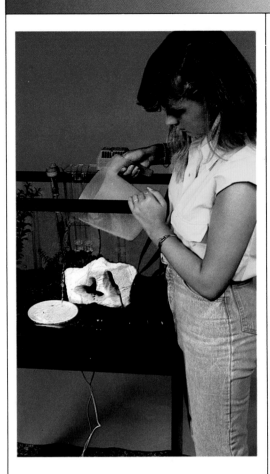

carefully! Once the heater has become slowly warmed up to the correct water temperature it is plugged in. Every automatic heater has a glowing control light, which indicates whether the heater is actually heating or whether it is in the *off* position. Unfortunately, this system is not uniformly adhered to by all manufacturers. In some heaters the lamp is on when it is heating, and in others it is on when it is not heating. Underwater heaters (submergibles) are also available at pet shops. Nevertheless, when the water is of the correct temperature all this is irrelevant.

We now adjust the control knob to the exact position where the lamp turns on and off. It really does not matter whether the instructions for it at the time of purchase. There are so many different makes and models of filters available that it is impossible to discuss all of them in detail. In any event, this should not pose a problem.

Now it is time to install the heater, preferably in a location where it does not affect the esthetics of the tank. This is easily achieved by camouflaging the heater with plants or other tank decorations. What is the temperature reading? Is this the correct water temperature? If this is so, the heater can be easily installed. The automatic heater should have been in the water (with the desired temperature) for about ten minutes, placed in an upright position with the control knob protruding above the water surface. If in doubt about anything, read the accompanying instructions

Be sure to add water to the tank very slowly. Even if this precaution is taken, however, some plants may become uprooted.

Artist's rendering of an action aerating ornament. Such decorative items are available at your local pet shop.

A plethora of pretty platies (*Xiphophorus maculatus*). The livebearing platy is peaceful by nature, therefore making it a wonderful community tank inhabitant.

"Now there will be an enormous temptation to immediately introduce the fish and turn on the aquarium illumination. I am only too aware of this, but we must be patient!"

heater is actually heating at that point or not; it will nevertheless maintain the present temperature. If at this stage you wish to change the temperature, it can easily be done. But any subsequent adjustment should be made in close consultation with the accompanying instructions provided by the manufacturer. Normally, one complete (clockwise) rotation of the control knob increases the temperature 1 to 4°C. When the knob is turned counter-clockwise there will be a corresponding temperature decrease.

At this stage our aquarium is completely set up. Now there will be an enormous temptation to immediately introduce the fish and turn on the aquarium illumination. I am only too aware of this, but we must be patient! Of course, it won't hurt to turn on the light for about ten minutes to see what everything looks like. In fact, we can go so far as to introduce the first few fish. Specifically, livebearers, such as guppies, platies or swordtails, can be put in the tank provided they are compatible with the master plan for that tank. Other species, however, are best kept out of the tank for the time being. Additionally, the "first arrivals" must not be fed yet. Please do not think for a moment that this is cruel; it is not! By their very nature tropical fish, indeed most fish, can occasionally fast for some time. Moreover, other edible items such as decaying plant leaves and stems and algae are often taken as substitute foods. Livebearers in general will eagerly feed on such plant (herbivorous) food. And that is what it is all about. These fish will then make sure that algae cannot become established in the tank. It is for that same reason that we must not turn on the tank light for extended periods, because initially this would only benefit the growth of algae. The higher plants, which are forming new roots now and will become properly established, do not usually need any light since they can survive from nutrients in their own system.

If anyone is indeed that impatient, he can turn the light on already, add all intended specimens and start feeding them; he may be lucky. Maybe it works out. But he must not be surprised when the entire interior of the aquarium (including substrate, plants and other decorations) soon becomes covered by an ugly green algal veil. This then inhibits the growth of the higher plants. It is indeed better to be patient for about five days. At that time all fish can be introduced into the

tank and the light turned on for good!

Major points of consideration for setting up an aquarium
*** Select the location
*** Establish fish stocking list and plant scheme
*** Test tank for leaks
*** Set up background
*** Do not forget tank support mat (felt, styrofoam, cardboard)
*** Wash sand and gravel
*** Place sand and gravel in tank
*** Gently add lukewarm water, about half of total tank volume

*** Position automatic heater and filter inside of tank. Do not plug in!
*** Plant bottom dwelling plants as per pre-determined scheme
*** Attach thermometer
*** Add rest of tank water, but monitor water temperature
*** Re-plant and/or secure plants which have become dislodged
*** If possible, "inoculate" aquarium and introduce

A swordtail (*Xiphophorus helleri*). Swordtails are variable in temperament— some are placid while others are aggressive.

Artist's rendering of an apple snail (*Ampullaria* species).

"Substrate bacteria may develop from a few 'seedlings' introduced into the aquarium via plant roots."

Artist's rendering of the trapdoor snail (*Melanoides tuberculata*).

burrowing snails
*** Introduce floating plants onto aquarium surface
*** Place lid over top of aquarium
*** Hold off with most fish, except a few livebearers. Do not turn on aquarium lights yet. Five days later turn on aquarium lights and execute aquarium stocking plan.

MORE USEFUL HINTS

Were you surprised when I recommended earlier that you "inoculate" a newly set-up aquarium? Now I would like to explain this in some detail.

All soil, be it in a garden or in a well-functioning (biologically balanced) aquarium, contains billions of tiny organisms, primarily *bacteria*. These organisms are everything but harmful. Quite the contrary; without soil bacteria, higher life forms could not exist. Therefore, an aquarium without substrate ("soil") bacteria would have only a limited life span. Either the entire community succumbs and is covered by a layer of algae, or bacteria populations will slowly develop anyway. But these bacteria do not appear out of thin air. Substrate bacteria populations may develop from a few "seedlings" introduced into the aquarium via plant roots. This process can take a long time and much can happen in the meantime. The "inoculation" specifically introduces a large

number of soil bacteria into the tank. This then helps to shorten the difficult lag period. An aquarium equipped with such microflora is generally referred to as being "run in" or "established." In such an aquarium the poisonous metabolic waste products from plants and animals are modified (i.e. oxidized) to less dangerous substances. Partial water changes at regular intervals will keep these substances at tolerable levels.

Where can we get such bacteria? If there is another, already established tank on hand, "inoculation" is not a problem. We take a few handfuls of substrate from the established tank and exchange this for fresh substrate from the new tank. This will not harm the established tank and it will most certainly benefit the new tank. Therefore, if we ever re-set up such a tank, the old substrate must never be thrown away! Instead, it is saved to be thoroughly washed in order to remove the dirt particles, but it is never treated with hot water! When aquarium soil is washed in cold or even lukewarm water a sufficient number of bacteria will survive to replenish the newly set-up tank.

If there is not any soil available from an established aquarium there is yet another method to "inoculate" an aquarium. For that purpose we immerse some garden soil (not recently fertilized!!) in a clean container and let this mixture stand for a few minutes. The supernatant clear or slightly cloudy water above the soil at the bottom is then poured into the aquarium. One way or the other it often

takes several weeks until an optimal bacterial flora has developed in our aquarium's substrate.

We must never add pure garden soil to our aquarium, because this can quickly lead to patches of decay in the substrate. Aquarium substrate—just as any other soil—should be loose (as opposed to compacted), so that fresh, oxygenated water can reach the roots of the plants. Otherwise these roots would die. This is also the reason for not using very fine sand for the aquarium, but instead fine to medium fine gravel. If the gravel is too coarse it creates problems. Earthworms continuously loosen and turn over garden soil. In our aquarium this task is taken over

by the Malayan burrowing snail (*Melanoides tuberculata*). As indicated by the name, it lives in the substrate, and because of its activity the soil remains permeable for water flow and patches of decay are avoided. These snails feed on dead organic particles and will not attack healthy plants. At night they sometimes come out of the soil and are visible along the bottom of the aquarium.

All other snails are either of no significance for our aquarium or they may even be outright dangerous. Their frequently advocated role as algae eaters is vastly over-rated. While members of the genera *Helisoma*, *Planorbis* and *Planorbarius* rarely ever cause problems, even in large numbers, an introduction of the mudsnail (*Lymnaea stagnalis*)

must be avoided. These snails are strongly herbivorous, feeding aggressively on water plants. Once any of them become noticeable in an aquarium, they must be manually (hand-picked) removed if we want to save the

The common pond snail (*Physa* species) is the snail most likely to become an aquarium nuisance.

Artist's rendering of the red ramshorn snail, a member of the genus *Planorbis*.

"We must never add pure garden soil to our aquarium, because this can quickly lead to patches of decay in the substrate."

Artist's rendering of one of several bottom-dwelling pond snails. These creatures feed on plants and algae. To be on the safe side, it is better to omit snails from the aquarium, at least at the beginning.

"If the leaves of aquarium plants turn yellow, there could be an iron deficiency in your aquarium."

aquarium plants. A word of caution, though: do not use chemicals to eradicate snails!! Damage caused to the plants could be far worse than any advantage in snail eradication.

Now a few words about fertilization and about the ways and means to allegedly improve water quality. Aquarium plants come from areas with greatly mineral-deficient water, which, for aquarium purposes, could only be provided by artificial means. Therefore, they have become adapted to getting by on mineral salts. Initially we should try to do without fertilizer substances because the partial water changes provide regular mineral supplements. In any event, fertilizer must never be added to a newly set-up tank because all it would do is enhance algal growth. It is important to know and appreciate that the ingredients of normal (garden and pot plant) fertilizers include large amounts of nitrogen. Nitrogen is a metabolic waste product and accumulates in excess in any aquarium. Consequently, we must not put normal fertilizer into our aquarium. For that reason the special fertilizer for aquarium plants should not contain any nitrogen; phosphorus should also be absent. As a final rule on this subject, rather than giving too much it is better not to use fertilizer at all in an aquarium!

If the leaves of aquarium plants turn yellow, there could be an iron deficiency in your aquarium. In this case, an exception should be made and special iron fertilizer added to the aquarium. Anyone who wants to do his plants a special favor can give them—apart from high illumination levels—carbon dioxide. Carbon dioxide supplement is an effective measure to enhance plant growth. Anyone who insists on having particularly beautiful plants should give some thought to purchasing one of the many

A pair of Madagascar rainbowfish (*Bedotia geayi*). Members of this species are active yet peaceful with their tankmates.

commercially available devices for carbon dioxide fertilization.

Also available from many pet and aquarium shops are various devices and chemical substances to improve the quality of aquarium water. Usually aquarium water bears little chemical resemblance to that from the native habitat of our fishes. Primarily, our water tends to be too hard and not acidic enough, but there are differences from one water supply to another. Water which is too hard can easily be softened through a dilution with demineralized water. Demineralizers are, however, expensive. Chlorinated water must not be used for filling an aquarium. Instead, it should be left standing for a few hours so that the chlorine can dissipate on its own.

In conclusion, I would like to address a mistake which is often made by beginning aquarists. Aquarium plants need 12 to 14 hours of light daily. They simply require this to sustain proper growth, and I would like to re-emphasize this very point. It is easy to believe the tank illumination is only there for the observer, and often aquarists do not turn the tank lights on until the evening hours. This problem is easily resolved by getting an electrical timing switch. It is not expensive and it makes sure that the tank light is automatically turned on and off. Plants as well as fish benefit from regular illumination. The light should be turned off late at night and turned on again about 13 hours later during the late morning hours or at noon. This way the aquarium is still fully illuminated during those hours when many of us are not at home.

BUYING THE FISH

Buying tropical fish is a matter of trust. A beginner is not in a position to judge either the health status or the suitability of fish. Instead, he has to rely solely on the dealer, who may also provide help and guidance when

"Plants as well as fish benefit from regular illumination. The light should be turned off late at night and turned on again about 13 hours later during the late morning hours or at noon."

Once we reach home the fish should be transferred into the aquarium as soon as possible. But remember, these new fish will have to adjust not only to another aquarium but also to other fish already present in the tank."

selecting pairs, as far as this is possible. It is fundamentally wrong just to take pot luck when buying fish. After all, we are responsible for our fish, even though they cost so little. There are many species which grow quite large, others may be incompatible and aggressive towards each other, and there are those which may feed on our plants. A layman would not know about this just by looking at the fish. Therefore, a novice (or any aquarist for that matter) must familiarize himself with the requirements of particular species *before* he goes through with the purchase.

Once the dealer has caught the fish they are packed carefully in plastic bags. We need not worry that the fish will suffocate in these watertight bags. Yet, care must be taken that, while in transit, nothing heavy is placed on the bag and that it does not cool off too much. Such a bag, well-wrapped in newspaper, will keep a sufficient temperature for at least an hour during the winter. During the summer the fish can be kept in such a bag in most instances for up to 24 hours. Of course, we do this only in an emergency, i.e. if the fish have to travel over a long distance.

Once we reach home the fish should be transferred into the aquarium as soon as possible. But remember, these new fish will have to adjust not only to another aquarium but also to

other fish already present in the tank. Moreover, water temperature and water condition in our aquarium will most likely be different from that in the plastic bag. Therefore, it is best to first "float" the still sealed bag on the water surface of the aquarium. This facilitates a temperature adjustment between aquarium water and that in the plastic bag over—let us say—15 minutes or so. If we notice, however, that our newly acquired fish continuously attempt to get out of the bag (and into the aquarium) we should let them go. In some fishes—and this includes swordtails—the stress of being restrained is apparently greater than the stress possibly caused by a significant temperature difference.

In order to let the fish out of the bag we open it and then gently and slowly permit the bag to fill up with water from the aquarium. It is important not to rush this process because slow mixing of water assures minimal stress among the fish still in the bag. In many cases it is obvious that the new arrivals are not very happy in their new surroundings. Their fins are closed and they tend to hide; often they are chased by the other fish. Yet, unless we made the wrong choice, we will soon notice that the newly arrived fish will settle in and become part of the fish community.

Care of The Aquarium

An aquarium is much less work than most people imagine. Once it is set up properly it can often be maintained for years with only minimal effort. Every day, at feeding time, check the thermometer and the filter. Everything OK? Then we can attend to the plants and fish in peace. Are they all feeding properly, with none of the fish hovering in one corner pale and with pinched fins? Diseased fish must be treated immediately. There are effective medications against the more common fish diseases. Similarly, we have to remove those specimens which are so constantly being chased by other fish that they are no longer able to feed properly. It goes without saying that dying and dead fish are taken out of the tank without delay. So our daily efforts are largely limited to careful monitoring, more or less as part of the daily feeding. As much as possible the plants are left undisturbed. If certain changes have to be made, these should be left until your monthly service.

MONTHLY SERVICE
Once a month there must be a major service of the aquarium. The very first thing we do is to pull out all—I repeat *all*—power plugs which lead to the aquarium from the outlet. Electrical current and water are a

A splendid Siamese fighting fish (*Betta splendens*).

Platies (*Xiphophorus maculatus*) and swordtails (*Xiphophorus helleri*) in a beautiful well-aerated aquarium.

"An aquarium is much less work than most people imagine. Once it is set up properly it can often be maintained for years with only minimal effort."

dangerous combination! The filter media are then thoroughly rinsed out and the filter cartridge washed out.

What is the appearance of the plants? Early on we were pleased about every new runner or shoot. But after a few months we have to start culling, i.e. cutting back some of the plant growth. If our tank is indeed well established, we may wish to replace some of the very fast growing plants with some which grow more slowly and are easier to keep. Maybe our stemmed plants have to be shortened. To do that, the new shoots are pinched off at the desired length and then simply planted at the desired spots. All these chores should be taken care of at this stage.

Now we proceed to a partial water change! For that we need a large plastic hose. One end is placed inside the tank and the other end downward into a bucket or—more conveniently— directly into a sink. Here it may pay to give some thought to buying a siphon hose several meters long to avoid carrying buckets and slopping water all over the floor. We suck briefly at the lower end of the hose and our aquarium starts to empty out. It is advisable to keep your hand always close to the suction end of the hose. This way we can instantly stop the water flow, e.g. when fish are in danger of getting sucked into the hose. At the same time we have maximum maneuverability of the hose and can direct it to any location in the tank where there is sediment. This dirt together with dead and decaying plant matter can easily be sucked up and removed from the aquarium in this manner.

As soon as a third of the tank's volume has been removed, suction should be stopped out of consideration for the fish, which may not be able to tolerate an excessive water change.

All that remains is cleaning the glass, in case green algae have started to settle there. Even in well-established tanks algae start to settle on the glass and the tank decorations. But this is not a disaster! On the contrary, the green algae indicate that the water quality is quite acceptable. These algae must not be mistaken for the ugly blue-green algae (which usually also appear greenish!) which often occur in newly set-up tanks.

Now replace the siphoned off water; the tank cover is put back, and all electrical appliances are plugged in again. It may yet be necessary to clean the outside of the glass with a regular window cleaner. Once this monthly service has been done a few times, it will eventually take less than 30 minutes to complete!

Red fighting fish (*Betta coccina*). This species is a recent icthyological discovery; it does not thrive in a community tank with other fishes, as it is rather shy.

How To Feed Your Fishes

Flake foods are among the most popular of the different dry fish foods on the market. They are available in many different formulations and package sizes. Photo courtesy of Hagen.

". . fish are far more active in nature and are less restricted in their movements than in a home aquarium. Therefore, many aquarists believe all fish should have one fasting day a week!"

Those times when you had to hike to the nearest pond with a water flea net in order to get food for your fish are over. Certainly, anyone wishing to keep and breed unusual fish may still have to do this sort of thing; in fact, most fish are grateful for the occasional live food. (By the way, some aquarists genuinely enjoy this sort of field excursion.) Most aquarists, though, will get their fish food from the nearest pet shop, even live foods.

There is a wide variety of fish food available, which includes dried food flakes, food tablets, freeze-dried foods, frozen foods and usually also live tubifex worms, *Daphnia* and bloodworms. Everything should be tried at some stage, but dried food flakes are usually the simplest.

OVER-FEEDING

Beginners particularly tend to make the mistake of over-feeding. After all, one wants to do the best one can for the fish, and they always look hungry as they come begging to the front glass! It is important for beginning aquarists to learn and appreciate the fact that most aquarium fish are excessively fat! This may not be visible externally in often slender-appearing specimens, but nevertheless, it is an established fact. In the wild, to which environment our fishes' metabolism is adapted, they tend to get very much less food than in our aquarium. Moreover, fish are far more active in nature and are less restricted in their movements than in a home aquarium. Therefore, many aquarists believe all fish should have one fasting day a week!

Over-feeding is also dangerous because uneaten food spoils the water or at least places an excessive burden on water quality. The consequence of this "fertilization" is rapid algae proliferation or an outright lethal water pollution. Therefore, all aquarists must remember this rule: never feed more than what is eaten by the fish within five minutes at the most! Anyone who adheres to this rule can do little else wrong. Uneaten food must always be removed from the tank.

There is also another point which must be remembered:

frozen food must always be thawed out before it is fed to the fish. By the way, if we really feel that our fish did not get enough at one feeding, we can feed again repeatedly in the course of a day. But the five-minute rule must always be observed.

WHAT TO DO DURING VACATION

And who is going to feed the fish during vacation? No problem! Even at the risk of surprising you—nobody! When there is nobody around (friend or neighbor) who is also an aquarist, it is better to leave the fish unattended. After all, even wild fish may have to fast for several weeks! At the completion of such a period they are often healthier than they were before. I usually arrange things as follows: the last few weeks before I go on vacation I do not purchase any new fish. The fish which are present are fed particularly well, also with live food. One day before my departure I adjust the automatic heater 4 to 5°C downward. This must be done one day before departure in order to ascertain

whether everything is working properly. Fish require much less food at lower temperatures, and it does not harm them.

I admit that my suggestion to let the fish fast may seem heartless, but it certainly does not represent cruelty to animals. However, anyone who does not have the heart to let the fish fast for a long period of time still has another opportunity to get them taken care of during vacation time. Specialized pet shops and aquarium shops offer so-called automatic feeders which can be installed and adjusted in such a way that they will dispense a suitable daily food ration to the fish.

While I am talking about the topic "vacation," one more point: even more important than an automatic feeder is an automatic light switch. Both of these can also be purchased as a single unit. Aquarium plants need 12 to 14 hours of light daily, not more, but also not very much less. If we do not meet this requirement, plant growth by the time we return from our holiday will have been abysmal!

Short-term automatic feeders are convenient for aquarists who have to be absent from home for a few days; long-term feeders, good for up to two weeks, are for vacationers. Photo courtesy of Aquarium Pharmaceuticals, Inc.

Frozen foods for aquarium use offer a wide variety of foodstuffs. Some are designed to appeal to aquarium fishes in general, and some are intended to have special appeal to individual groups of fishes such as vegetarian species. Photo courtesy of Ocean Nutrition.

Fish Diseases

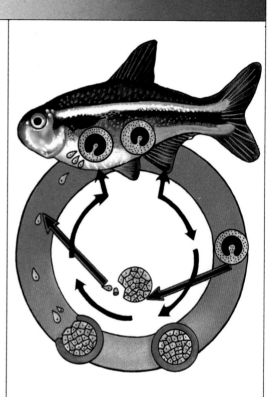

"Fish, like any other organisms, can become sick. This can be recognized in behavioral changes. They are no longer actively swimming about; maybe they remain in one corner with folded fins and with their body wobbling; maybe they have a rash on the body and fins."

Aeromonas bacteria infect a fish and eat away at the tissue, producing an area that looks as if it had rotted away.

Artist's rendering of the life cycle of white spot disease. Ich organisms can infect and reinfect the tank if they are not wiped out as early on as possible.

Fish, like any other organisms, can become sick. This can be recognized in behavioral changes. They are no longer actively swimming about; maybe they remain in one corner with folded fins and with their body wobbling; maybe they have a rash on the body and fins. When

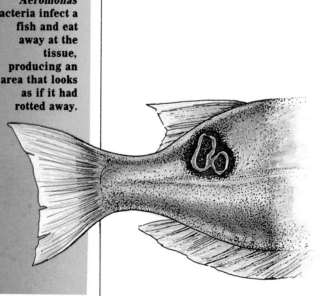

we see these signs we must immediately check the thermometer. Or could it be that the water has gone bad?

This is sufficient cause to take a very close look at the fish. Are there a few white dots in fins and body? If so, then it may be a case of *Ichthyophthirius* (ich or white spot disease), the most common freshwater fish disease. If nothing is done quickly, the entire fish stock will be wiped out. Pet shops do have medications for sale which are 100% effective, so there is no need to panic! When one fish shows these symptoms, others—possibly all of them—have the disease too. The medication must be given directly into the aquarium. The accompanying instructions must be followed closely. If we have acted in time, the disease will be controlled. Therefore, it is of paramount importance that the fish are frequently examined for the dreaded white spots!

Somewhat more difficult to diagnose is *Oodinium* (velvet). This disease also manifests itself by the presence of whitish or brownish dots, but they are very much smaller than for ich and one has to look very closely to detect them. In the advanced stage this disease takes the form of a velvet-like coating over the skin. Fish with this disease are more easily recognized by a change in their behavior: reluctance to feed, folded fins, and tendency to hide. The treatment and medication can be provided by your pet shop. If fish are kept at temperatures which are too low, there is the possibility that fungus may occur. This too will rapidly respond to the proper medication, and the same applies to fin rot. Chewed up or lost fins can also be due to biting by other specimens. Therefore, it is important that the fish are closely monitored.

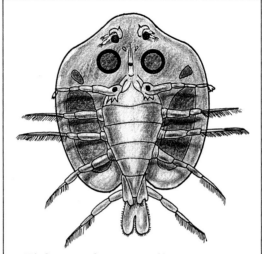

Fish can also get a disease which cannot be treated successfully, or treated only under particularly favorable circumstances. Specimens with an obviously swollen abdomen, caved-in abdomen or severely distended eyes must be immediately taken out and isolated so that the pathogens are not transferred to other tank occupants. Also remember that

Artist's rendering of the ventral view of the fish louse (*Argulus*).

"Specimens with an obviously swollen abdomen, caved-in abdomen or severely distended eyes must be immediately taken out and isolated so that the pathogens are not transferred to other tank occupants."

Signs of a healthy fish. If you are in doubt about a certain specimen's condition, don't buy it.

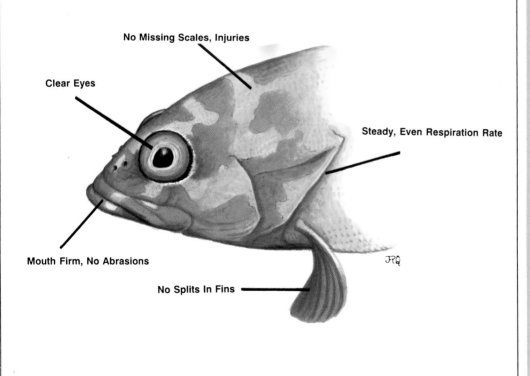

No Missing Scales, Injuries

Clear Eyes

Steady, Even Respiration Rate

Mouth Firm, No Abrasions

No Splits In Fins

somewhere along the line the normal life expectancy for a particular species and specimen comes to a normal end. A few species reach a maximum age of only one or two years, while most of our small tropical fish may get to be only three to five years old. If your interest lies in tropical fish diseases, there are lots of books on the subject available at your local aquarium store.

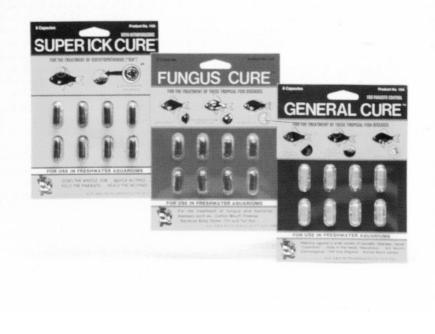

Your local aquarium dealer will stock many different types of preventives (upper photo) and medications (lower photo) that are effective against many common—and some not-so-common— diseases that attack aquarium fishes. Photos courtesy of Aquarium Pharmaceuticals, Inc.

Community Tanks

The molly (*Poecilia sphenops*) varies in its suitability as a community fish—some are peaceful while others are quite aggressive.

A *community tank* is simply a tank with fish and plants which get along well together. Here it does not matter to the hobbyist whether the tank has only fish from South America together with water plants from the same continent. Instead, the tank can also contain fishes from Southeast Asia or Africa. The important thing is that the tank looks attractive and the fishes are compatible. This is by far the most common type of aquarium among aquarists. Here we are not going to deal with special tanks or even breeding tanks.

The experienced aquarist can think of a multitude of possibilities to set up community tanks and to combine various fish and plant species. But without an adequate knowledge about the variable requirements of plants and animals, the novice may end up paying dearly for his ignorance. Therefore, I would like to take this opportunity to discuss some of the most important factors that have to be taken into consideration. Then I will make a detailed proposal

Bleeding heart tetras (*H. erythrostigma*) are active fish that need lots of room. They are peaceful in the community tank if kept with fishes of their own size.

43

"...those plants
which do not
take up a lot of
space are
planted in
groups. This
looks more
appealing than
a random
scattering of
plants
throughout the
aquarium."

about the actual setup, one which I consider to be most suitable. This is followed by a stocking list of fish species which are relatively easy to keep, but which are also particularly attractive and very interesting at the same time. With this our aquarium can never be boring!

SETTING UP THE TANK

First of all, there are some fundamentals about setting up a community tank which go beyond what has already been said.

We need a lot of rapidly growing plants. These are usually cheap. They can be replaced with more demanding plants later on. Our first planting scheme must be appealing, so those plants which do not take up a lot of space are planted in groups. This looks far more appealing than a random scattering of plants throughout the aquarium. Low-growing plants are placed more towards the front and taller plants along the sides and in the background. A particularly large plant should give the tank a certain highlight and focal point. It is planted as a solitary plant and should be given a conspicuous position in the tank layout. But so that it does not look too deliberate and artificial, this position must not be dead center in the tank, but instead off-center to the right or left.

It goes without saying that the individual light requirements of the plant species must be given careful consideration. Other than that, we should attempt to arrange the groups of plants in some sort of contrasting pattern. For instance, put plants with stems next to bottom dwellers, delicate ones next to those with sturdy leaves, green plants next to those with a reddish

**A trio of zebra
danios
(*Brachydanio
rerio*).**

A pair of platies (*Xiphophorus maculatus*).

"Some fish species are typically solitary and should be kept at best with a partner of the opposite sex."

A pair of swordtails (*Xiphophorus helleri*).

coloration, etc.

Now to the fish. Here too our primary consideration must deal with their specific requirements. Their decorative value must come second. How can we enjoy our fish if they are obviously not feeling well? Basically, we distinguish between those species which prefer soft water and those which like the water somewhat harder. Most tropical species come from soft-water regions, from the rain forests of South America, from Africa and southern Asia. They require relatively soft water, which may not always be readily accessible to us. But this does not represent a problem, because there are a number of species which can adapt quite readily to our tap water. Many species have been bred in our water for many generations, and these are the only ones recommended here. The more difficult species should be acquired only after some experience with fish has been gained. Nevertheless, every aquarist should know whether his water is soft, medium or hard.

Setting up the tank is the same. Some fish species are typically solitary and should be kept at best with only a partner of the opposite sex. Regrettably, that too represents problems at times; yet these are the types of fish which are particularly interesting in their behavior.

They establish a territory, and anyone who is successful in mating a pair of such territorial fish can observe their highly fascinating family life. Since most aquarists would like to have fish like that, I have included a pair of such territorial fish in my community tank stocking list.

Schooling fish are much easier to keep in groups. In fact, they feel really well only in each other's company. There is nothing worse that you can do to a schooling fish than to keep it alone. These fish require many others around them, not only one or two or three—a school should not be less than at least five, preferably more!

Novice aquarists are often tempted to put as many different fish together as possible. Please resist this temptation! An

"Schooling fish are much easier to keep in groups. In fact, they feel really well only in each other's company. There is nothing worse that you can do to a schooling fish than to keep it alone."

Cherry barbs (*Capoeta titteya*) are a favorite community tank species. They are highly recommended for the beginner.

aquarium with fewer species and not too many specimens is more interesting than one which is absolutely loaded with fish. Every fish needs a certain space in order to develop normally and to display its qualities. From an esthetic point of view it is also more appealing to have two large schools of fish in a tank rather

"Every fish needs a certain space in order to develop normally and to display its qualities. From an esthetic point of view it is also more appealing to have two large schools of fish in a tank rather than five little ones."

The lyretail lamprologus (*Lamprologus brichardi*) is one of many species that needs a rocky tank set-up to feel completely at home.

than five little ones.

Gravel and rocks: In order to be able to set up our tank we need—apart from sand or gravel—a few rocks. Before the (washed) gravel is added to the tank the rocks are put in place. They are positioned directly on the glass bottom, so that they cannot be burrowed under by (and collapse on top of) some fish. One large rock should reach almost to the surface, but it must be fairly flat so that it does not take up too much space. A piece of roofing slate would be ideal for that purpose. It is placed in the left back corner as camouflage for the inside filter. After all, as useful as a filter is, it is not an esthetic masterpiece! The rock plate is supported laterally against the aquarium wall. So that it does not slide away it is further supported at the bottom with another good-sized rock. The latter will be covered by the substrate so that it is no longer visible. A second, smaller piece of slate is placed at an angle against the larger one. This reduces the artificial appearance of this arrangement, and simultaneously it provides a cave, which is essential for cichlids. The other rocks are arranged on the right side of the tank. Essentially they are to separate a shallow layer of gravel in the foreground from a higher one behind the rocks. This way a terrace is created, giving our aquarium greater visual depth when the substrate rises from the front to the back.

All rocks are placed directly onto the bottom. Then sand or gravel is added. This sand or gravel layer should be at least 3 cm deep along the front glass and 5 to 8 cm in the back of the tank. The far right corner is filled up with a root. This is a significant decorative element in the tank, and it should extend all the way to the water surface. In doing so

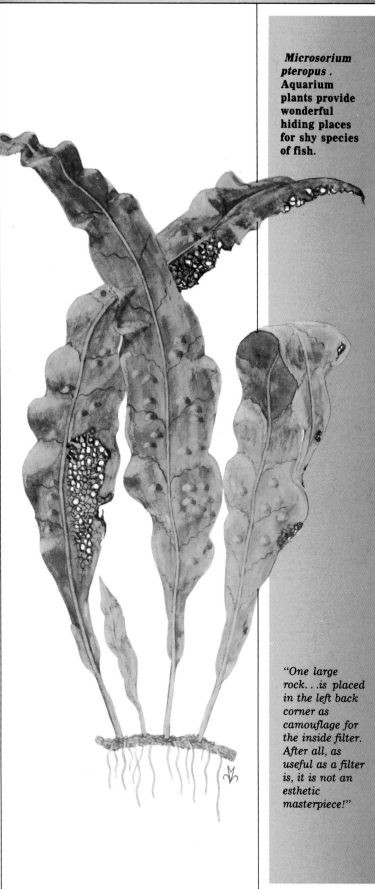

Microsorium pteropus. Aquarium plants provide wonderful hiding places for shy species of fish.

"One large rock. . .is placed in the left back corner as camouflage for the inside filter. After all, as useful as a filter is, it is not an esthetic masterpiece!"

Left: Dwarf Amazon swordplant (*Echinodorus tenellus*). *Right:* One of the water milfoils (*Myriophyllum spicatum*).

"Water plants—apart from their biological significance—are also important items for our aquarium. Even the very first planting will provide a very visually appealing aquarium."

it camouflages the automatic heater and at the same time affords hiding places for surface fishes as well as for bottom dwellers. It also provides an anchorage for floating plants.

Planting scheme: Water plants—apart from their biological significance—are also important decorative items for our

aquarium. Even the very first planting will provide a very visually appealing aquarium.

First I would like to give you a list of plants which are *absolutely essential*. The common name is listed before the scientific designation, which can also be helpful when the plants are purchased. All plants listed here are common and should be available from all aquarium shops. They are all inexpensive

"It does not hurt to get two or three extra plants of each species. Only the centerpiece plant, the Amazon swordplant, should be represented by a single plant."

plants, so get as many as required. The numbers following the name indicate approximately how many individual plants should be purchased. It does not hurt to get two or three extra plants of each species. Only the centerpiece plant, the Amazon swordplant, should be represented by a single plant.

PLANTS WITH STEMS—*Hygrophila polysperma*, three to five; water wisteria *(Hygrophila difformis)*, three to four; Ludwigia *(Ludwigia spec.)*, four to five.

PLANTS WHICH LIVE CLOSE TO THE SUBSTRATE—corkscrew Vallisneria *(Vallisneria spiralis)*, seven to ten; Amazon swordplant *(Echinodorus* species), one; Cryptocoryne *(Cryptocoryne affinis)*, five to ten; Java fern *(Microsorium pteropus)*, two to four; dwarf arrowplant *(Sagittaria subulata pusilla)*, four to six.

FLOATING PLANTS—water sprite *(Ceratopteris thalicroides)*, one.

The numbers given in this list can, of course, only be guidelines. They refer to large to medium size individual plants and a 100-liter aquarium. If plants are bought in small plastic

Vallisneria spiralis portugalensis. Members of this species are sometimes called wild celery or eel grass.

51

"One corner in the foreground should be planted with Sagittaria subulata pusilla, which attains a height of only 5 to 10 cm. Its abundant runners will soon cover the foreground like a lawn."

cups, correspondingly fewer are required, and they usually are the best quality.

In the event that some species are not available, here are some examples of substitutes; the water wisteria can be replaced by *Hygrophila stricta* or *Hygrophila corymbosa;* for *Vallisneria spiralis,* substitute *Vallisneria asiatica biwaensis;* for the Amazon swordplant, the red

Right: One of the several "false loosestrife" plants, *Ludwigia palustris. Left:* This "crypt" (*Cryptocoryne wendtii*) comes from Sri Lanka.

tiger lotus *(Nymphaea lotus); Cryptocoryne affinis* can be substituted with *C. wendtii;* and instead of water sprite use horned sprite *(Ceratopteris cornuta).*

One corner in the foreground should be planted with *Sagittaria subulata pusilla,* which attains a height of only 5 to 10 cm. Its abundant runners will soon cover the foreground like a lawn. After one month plant growth will have changed substantially. The stemmed plants will have grown upward and produced branches; the corkscrews will have many runners and the Amazon swordplant will have spread out. This is the sign that the aquarium has passed the critical phase and we can now start to gradually change the tank. Have the *Vallisneria* already produced strong runners behind the large rock? If so, we should then restrict them to that area. Then, where the *Vallisneria* used to grow, we can plant some delicate *Myriophyllum*. Alternatively, shoots from the *Hygrophila*

Right: **One of the *Barclayas* (*Barclaya longifolia*).** *Left:* **This species, *Ludwigia arcuata*, comes from Virginia and Florida.**

polysperma, which by now may be closing in on the Amazon swordplant, can be planted there. The water wisteria is then thinned out by simply pinching off several shoots and pushing these into the substrate. Later on we can establish an attractive colony of *Rotala macrantha* at this spot. The Cryptocorynes should be left alone. They should be left alone because only then

"After one month plant growth will have changed substantially.

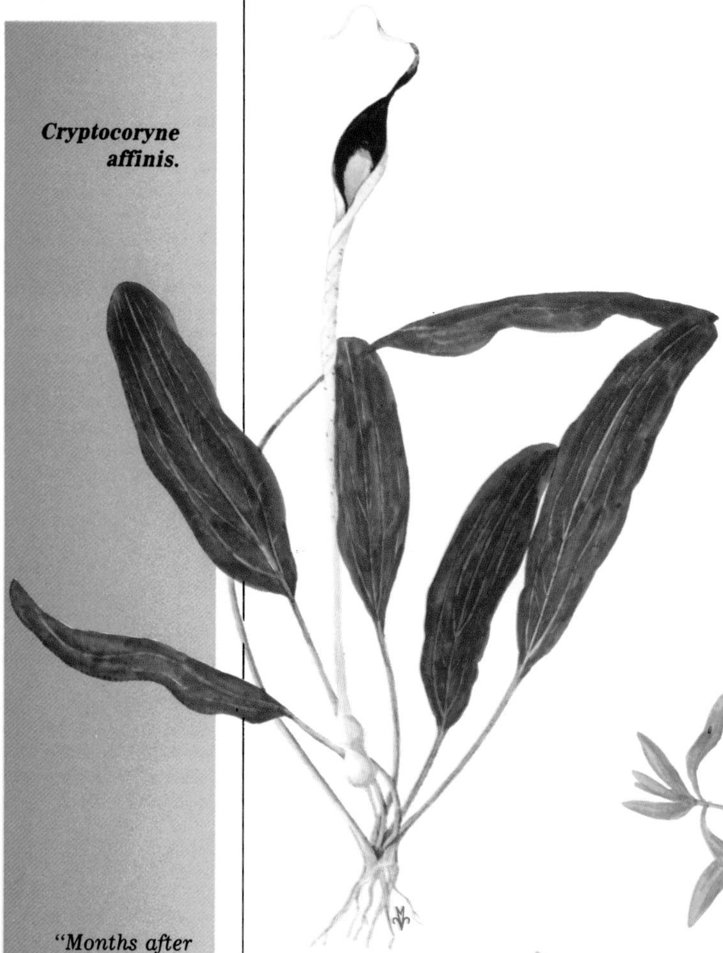

Cryptocoryne affinis.

"Months after the tank has been set up we can also introduce more demanding plant species than Sagittaria subulata pusilla *as the foreground cover."*

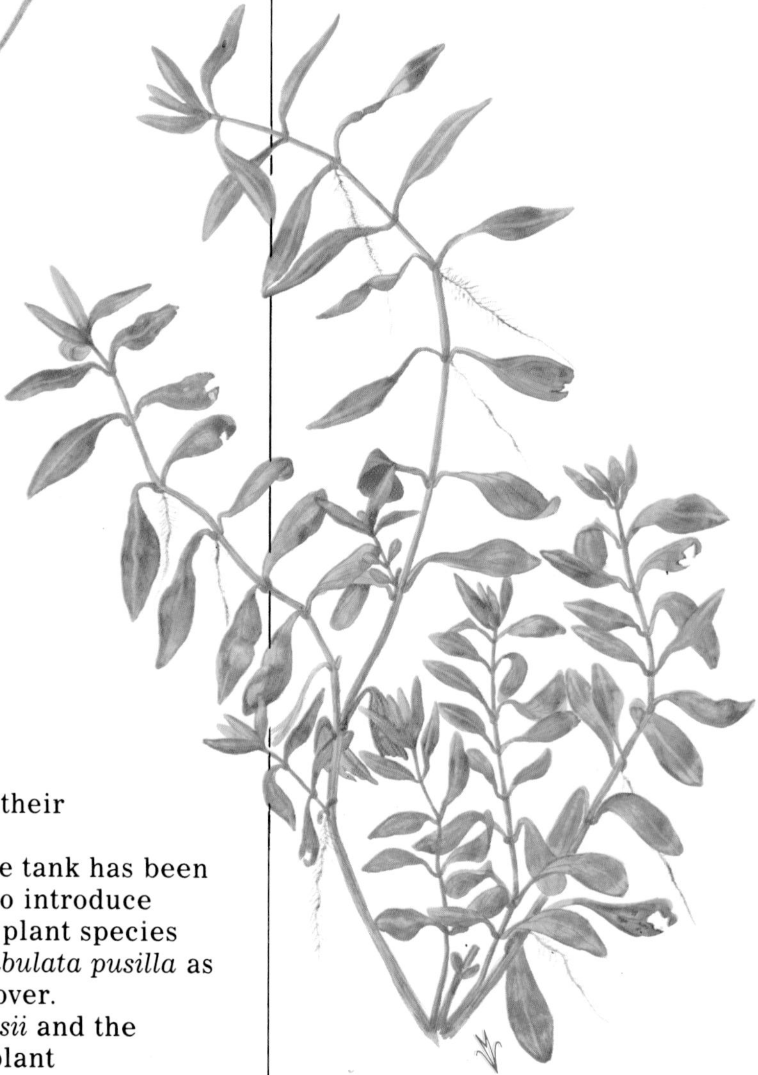

Hygrophila polysperma.

Echinodorus tenellus are suitable for the left half of the tank. Both species must be kept undisturbed, but given sufficient time and if care is taken that the floating plants do not keep too much light from them, both may develop into rather attractive underwater carpets.

The above example has been designed for a 100-liter tank. Adapting this to an 80-liter tank is not difficult. In fact, we

will they display their robustness.

Months after the tank has been set up we can also introduce more demanding plant species than *Sagittaria subulata pusilla* as the foreground cover. *Cryptocoryne willisii* and the grass-like swordplant proceed exactly the same way, and as far as plant numbers are concerned we simply select the lower of the range numbers listed for a particular species. The Amazon swordplant may be getting a bit too large after a few months. We can then replace it with an equally effective but slower growing solitary plant, e.g. *Barclaya*. It is not recommended, however, that this sensitive plant be used for start-up planting.

The adaptation of my decorating scheme to a 200-liter tank is simpler yet. Of course, we do require a few more plants, but not twice the numbers! About a third more plants should be sufficient, and of course we stick with a single solitary centerpiece.

"The Amazon swordplant may be getting a bit too large after a few months. We can then replace it with an equally effective but slower growing solitary plant, e.g. Barclaya. It is not recommended, however, that this sensitive plant be used for start-up planting."

Water wisteria (*Hygrophila difformis*).

This *Cryptocoryne* species (*Cryptocoryne willisii*) is now commonly known as *Cryptocoryne axelrodi.*

Rotala macrantha is a rather slow-growing plant. It is often cultivated with *Cryptocoryne.*

One of the fanworts (*Cabomba aquatica*).

One of the dwarf Amazon swordplants (*Echinodorus quadricostatus*).

A pair of aeneus catfish (*Corydoras aeneus*). This species is one of the armoured catfishes, named for the hard bony plates which protect them against larger fish.

"I know the temptation is great to include a few cardinal tetras and a pair of angelfish, as well as a few colorful dwarf cichlids and some gobies. Please resist this temptation, at least for a while yet."

Chinese algae-eater (*Gyrinocheilus aymonieri*). Despite its common name, this species actually comes from Thailand.

FISH FOR A COMMUNITY TANK

Now we are coming to the fish; here I suggest particularly attractive, rather active and interesting fish which do not require excessive care. There should be no difficulties at all with the combination suggested below. The optimal temperature is about 24°C (75°F). The first number refers to a 100-liter tank. The numbers in brackets refer to an 80-liter aquarium.

COMBINATION A—zebra danios (*Brachydanio rerio*), ten [seven] fish; head and tail light tetras (*Hemigrammus ocellifer*), ten [seven] fish; platies (*Xiphophorus maculatus*), five [four] fish; dusky kribs (*Pelvicachromis pulcher*), one pair; Siamese flying fox (*Epalzeorhynchus siamensis*), one fish.

I know the temptation is great to include a few cardinal tetras and a pair of angelfish, as well as a few colorful dwarf cichlids and some gobies. Please resist this temptation, at least for a while yet. The species suggested will provide fascinating viewing pleasure for a very long time, and all of them are easily available. Should some be unavailable they can be replaced with others; e.g. instead of zebra danios select cherry barbs (*Capoeta titteya*); instead of head and tail light tetras we can choose flame tetras (*Hyphessobrycon flammeus*), and

Epalzeorhynchus stigmaeus is closely related to the Siamese flying fox (*E. siamensis*).

"*I would suggest that if you must add fish, just add another two or three zebra danios and the head and tail light tetras.*"

A trio of McCulloch's rainbowfish (*Melanotaenia maccullochii*).

red platies can easily be replaced with red swordtails. The Chinese algae eater (*Gyrinocheilus aymonieri*) is an excellent replacement for the Siamese flying fox (*Epalzeorhynchus siamensis*). These species are easily interchangeable.

For a 200-liter aquarium you cannot simply double the number of fishes suggested for a 100-gallon tank. While a few extra plants are still acceptable, stocking an extra large tank with fish requires some self-control. I would suggest that if you must add fish, just add another two or three of the zebra danios and the head and tail light tetras. Furthermore, you can also purchase a small group of the cute little *Corydoras* catfish, preferably either *Corydoras paleatus* or *Corydoras aeneus*. Most of the other *Corydoras* species are somewhat more demanding in respect to care. About six of them would be the right number. However, these

fishes require fine sand. If we started out with a gravel substrate, we can still correct this problem. In one of the plant-free zones close to the front of the tank we replace an area approximately the size of an eight-inch saucer with thoroughly washed fine sand. The gravel which we have removed can be scattered along the bottom in the back of the tank. We thus have

Adolfo's catfish. Female *Corydoras* catfish are wider in body than the males.

Adolfo's catfish (*Corydoras adolfoi*). The dish containing tubifex worms is set up for two reasons: 1) to keep the tubifex confined until eaten so they don't establish themselves in the tank substrate; 2) to provide separate provisions for the catfish who, as bottom dwellers, don't get enough to eat during regular feedings, as the fish closest to the top gets there first.

"What do we do if the tap water is too hard (20° total hardness or more)? In this case we have to slightly modify the fish inventory."

built a little "sand box" for the catfish, which they are certainly going to use.

What do we do if the tap water is too hard (20° total hardness or more)? In this case we have to slightly modify the fish inventory.

COMBINATION B—McCullogh's

rainbowfish *(Melanotaenia macullochii),* ten [seven] fish; red swordtail *(Xiphophorus helleri),* one male or two [one] females; black mollies *(Poecilia sphenops),* two pairs; dusky kribs *(Pelvicachromis pulcher),* one pair; Chinese algae eater *(Gyrinocheilus aymonieri),* one fish.

If the dwarf rainbowfish are not available we can add a school of Madagascar rainbowfish *(Bedotia geayi)* instead. Again, the figures in brackets are for an 80-liter tank. For a 200-liter tank, we can enlarge the fish inventory with a small school (five to six fish) of red rainbowfish, *Glossolepis incisus.*

Ember tetras *(H. amandae).* Members of this genus prefer to school with fish of the same species but may sometimes school with other genus mates.

Leopard danios
(*Brachydanio
frankei*).

Boeseman's
rainbowfish
(*Melanotaenia
boesemani*) is a
good
community
fish if it it kept
in schools and
in a large, wide
tank.

Red rainbowfish (*Glossolepis incisus*). This species is also known as the New Guinea rainbowfish.

A pair of platies (*Xiphophorus maculatus).* The male platy is smaller and slimmer than the female. The male of this pair is the upper fish.

A Miniature Aquarium

SETTING UP AND SELECTING FISH

There can be no doubt that a 100-liter tank is better than a 40-liter tank, especially for a beginner. But for young people, getting the larger tank is often too costly, especially since the initial purchase will have to include a tank light, an automatic heater, and a filter. There is, however, an inexpensive alternative!

Let us choose a smaller tank with a volume of about 20 to 40 liters. We can do without a filter and really do not need a special tank light, but we do need at least

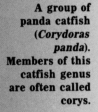

"There can be no doubt that a 100-liter tank is better than a 40-liter tank, especially for a beginner. But for young people, getting the larger tank is often too costly. . ."

A pair of aeneus catfish (*Corydoras aeneus*).

a desk lamp! We have to stick to the required illumination times—13 to 14 hours each day. Another piece of equipment we cannot do without is an automatic heater. A 30-liter tank needs a 30-watt heater.

The tank is set up principally the same as I have described for larger tanks. Therefore, do *not* skimp on plants! In spite of its small size, even such a tank can be nicely structured to provide ample hiding places. It is suitable for rather diverse fish species. If this is going to be a first aquarium, the aquarist is advised to settle for hardy, resistant fish, especially in a miniature tank. After all, it is in these small tanks that the water quality can deteriorate much faster than in larger tanks. This can become dangerous for more sensitive fish, in spite of regular water changes.

Therefore, I suggest a fish inventory of species which have an accessory breathing organ in addition to gill respiration, which enables them to take oxygen directly from the air. These are the labyrinth fishes. They have a multi-branched, air-filled cavity covered by their gill covers, the so-called *labyrinth organ*. These fishes swim up to the surface regularly in order to exhale the used air from this organ and to take in fresh (oxygenated) air. This unique ability enables them to survive in their native habitats in southern Asia in oxygen-deficient swamps without any difficulties.

Catfish also use accessory

"If this is going to be a first aquarium, the aquarist is advised to settle for hardy, resistant fish, especially in a miniature tank."

"Not all species of labyrinth fishes are suitable for our minitank. Some simply get too large, while others are excessively sensitive fish."

respiration. They swallow air and remove the oxygen in their digestive tract. But not all species are easy to keep. The two most suitable species are the spotted corydoras *(Corydoras paleatus* and *Corydoras aeneus)*. As a small school (about five fish) they can easily inhabit the bottom region of the minitank, if we make sure that there are at

(Macropodus opercularis); Siamese fighting fish *(Betta splendens)* are also ideal. However, both of these are territorial fish. We can select only one of the two and then only one male and one female. If we now wish to breed them we must also do without the catfish. Which one of the labyrinth fish should we select? Both species are attractive as

A pair of paradise fish (*Macropodus opercularis*) spawning beneath a bubblenest.

least some patches of fine sand. However, stick with one species of *Corydoras!*

   Not all species of labyrinth fishes are suitable for our minitank. Some simply get too large, while others are excessively sensitive fish. The most suitable species for such minitanks are paradise fish

well as hardy and easily available. Paradise fish have the advantage that they can even be kept without a heater in rooms which are sufficiently warm. This is an important point to consider when young are to be raised.

BREEDING PARADISE FISH
   I know a few students who

A group of panda catfish (*Corydoras panda*) eating tubifex worms from a special feeder.

made some extra pocket money breeding paradise fish. Of course, nobody gets rich doing that, but that is not really the purpose. The pleasure of breeding and rearing the fish is far more important.

Paradise fish were among the first tropical fish kept in home aquaria. They prefer a temperature range from 20° to 28°C (68 to 82°F). For general maintenance a normally heated room is sufficient during the winter. Only on occasion should the temperature be allowed to drop below 18°C (65°F); successful breeding requires water temperatures from about 25° to 27°C (77 to 81°F). Then, of course, we cannot do without a heater.

The breeding tank is set up the same as the minitank just discussed. Neither aeration nor filtration is desired, because the male paradise fish builds a floating nest made of many tiny air bubbles at the surface. This

"I know a few students who made some extra pocket money breeding paradise fish. Of course, nobody gets rich doing that, but that is not really the purpose. The pleasure of breeding and rearing the fish is far more important."

A giant gourami (*Colisa fasciata*) tending to its bubblenest. *Colisa* species like to anchor the bubblenest to a floating plant.

*Paradise fish (**Macropodus opercularis**) tending to its bubblenest.*

"Dried food alone is not going to bring us superior breeding results. The best conditioning foods are live bloodworms, glassworms and mosquito larvae in sufficient quantities."

*A pair of Siamese fighting fish (**Betta splendens**). As you can see, members of this species come in several colors.*

delicate structure could easily be destroyed by excessive water movements. The tank should be well-planted. It should also contain a tall rock (in a vertical position) or a piece of driftwood which reaches all the way to the surface. This helps the female to get to the surface unmolested by the male, because she must surface regularly to breathe. This precaution is necessary because during the nest-building period the male is extremely aggressive, even towards his own female. She needs lots of hiding places (plant thickets, some cave structures, etc.) to keep out of sight of the male.

We must not forget to include floating plants in such an aquarium. They serve to support the bubble nest as well as provide an environment for the myriads of microscopically small organisms which are the first food for young paradise fish. The first thing we must do is to bring the adult pair into breeding condition with a proper diet. Dried food alone is not going to bring us superior breeding results. The best conditioning foods are live bloodworms, glassworms and

mosquito larvae in sufficient quantities. These will quickly stimulate egg production in the female. But it is not always easy to get this sort of food. Pet shops and aquarium shops often have this sort of live food. If all fails we can also use frozen bloodworms and mosquito larvae. These are usually available from pet shops.

High temperatures, no water movement, suitable food in sufficient quantities, adequate hiding places for the female—if we take all these points into consideration, breeding paradise fish should not be a problem. If we comply with all these points the male will soon start building his bubble nest. Maybe if we are lucky we can watch the pair spawn. At that point the female can move freely under the nest without being driven off by the male. Quite to the contrary, now the male will repeatedly drape his body around that of the female. Then we can see the slightly cloudy eggs rising up to the nest in large numbers, often in small clumps. Eggs that drift away are usually retrieved by the male and returned to the nest. Sometimes the female helps him with this task.

Spawning is usually completed within a few hours, and then the female is no longer allowed to be close to the nest. In fact, she is often driven off again by the male. Therefore, it is best to remove the female once spawning has been completed. Transfer her to a separate small tank (plastic aquarium). A five-liter tank would be sufficient. It does not need to be planted, but we must assure that the female receives a proper diet; after all, we may wish to breed her again in a few weeks' time.

The eggs and young are now guarded exclusively by the male, which stops taking food for the duration of guarding the nest and young. The young will hatch in about 28 hours. We have to look very closely in order to recognize them at all. They hang like tiny whitish commas in the nest. They start to swim from about the third or fourth day after spawning. Then they take up a horizontal position and are quite capable of maintaining themselves motionless in the open water

since by then they have a functional swim bladder. Now the time has come to remove the male from the breeding tank too. Just like the female, he will be placed in a separate tank—but not with the female.

Things become a bit tricky if you miss the spawning altogether. Then the nest has to

be checked every day for the presence of the white (about 1 mm in diameter) eggs or possibly larvae. By then, of course, it will be high time to remove the female. Often it is easier to detect the eggs simply by closely watching the male, because it is hard to distinguish between mere air bubbles and the eggs or larvae inside the nest.

"Spawning is usually completed within a few hours, and then the female is no longer allowed to be close to the nest. In fact, she is often driven off again by the male."

A Siamese fighting fish tending to its bubblenest. Both the Siamese fighting fish and the paradise fish become even more aggressive than usual during the spawning season.

Brine shrimp eggs. Newly hatched *Artemia* are a staple for rearing young fry.

A vivid blue Siamese fighting fish (*Betta splendens*).

"Once the young paradise fish are swimming about freely, they need food without delay. They are so small that they cannot feed on regular fish food."

Spawning paradise fish (*Macropodus opercularis*).

Nevertheless, the first spawning is easily overlooked, because it is hard for a novice to imagine how small the eggs and larvae actually are. A labyrinth fish enthusiast told me that he had been unable to breed his fish. When I then looked into his tank I saw a large number of young fish swimming just below the surface. The hobbyist had overlooked them completely!

Rearing the young: Once the young paradise fish are swimming about freely, they need food without delay. They are so small that they cannot feed on regular fish food. Fortunately, every well-established aquarium contains a multitude of tiny organisms called *infusoria*. These serve as the first food for the young paradise fish. But in our small tank there are certainly not enough infusoria for all of the 300 to 500 fish larvae; we would be happy if we could rear only a fraction of them.

After a week the young will be large enough to feed on *Artemia*. These are brine shrimp, which are available in the form of eggs from pet shops. Once these eggs are returned to a saline solution the small nauplii larvae will

hatch out within about two days. To do this we fill a plastic dish with one liter of water, add a level teaspoon of non-iodized salt as well as a pinch of *Artemia* eggs. This mixture is stirred well, and all you do then is wait. The hatched nauplii larvae are attracted by light and will congregate at the illuminated side of the dish. They are easily recognized by their orange-reddish coloration. They can be siphoned out of the dish with a small-diameter hose (standard air hose available from all pet shops!) and are then placed directly into the breeding tank.

Anyone who wants to be a bit more professional about this can buy himself an aerator and a brine shrimp hatchery. This device increases the yield of hatching nauplii quite substantially. Both the brine shrimp hatchery and *Artemia* eggs come complete with detailed instructions. Follow these instructions carefully.

As soon as the young *Macropodus* start feeding on *Artemia* larvae, they are over the

worst. From that point on their growth is quite rapid, and the aquarist should soon try some finely ground up dried food sprinkled on the water surface. A word of caution though: remember that uneaten food fouls the water!

There is yet another food source; anybody who has seen how fast the young will grow and how aggressively they will feed on this food will not want to do without it. Most pet shops sell live *Tubifex* worms. These are small red worms, but at their full

size they are still too large for young paradise fish and so they will have to be chopped up! In order to be able to do this efficiently a small clump of *Tubifex* is placed on a piece of cardboard and then cut into small pieces—like parsley—with a razor blade. This "worm mash" is an excellent fish rearing food.

Soon thereafter the young paradise fish will take whole *Tubifex* and, of course, dried food. Regular water changes, apart from a proper diet, are also essential for rapid growth.

Consequently, it is advantageous to make partial water changes more frequently. To change a third of the tank volume every third or fourth day is not too much. Of course, much care has to be taken not to siphon out any of the small paradise fish. Here is a hint to avoid accidental sucking up of young fish: use a foam rubber cartridge, as used in inside filters. It can be slipped over the suction end of the hose and will prevent any of the young from getting into the hose.

Breeding Siamese fighting fish is similar, although they require a temperature of about 25°C (77°F). Moreover, the young will have to be separated once they have reached a size of about 10 mm. At that size they can be placed inside jam jars or similar containers. The temperature can be maintained by placing the jars into a water bath where a constant temperature is being maintained with an automatic heater. Breeding Siamese fighting fish is particularly interesting because of their multitude of color strains.

Paradise fish are perhaps the easiest fish to breed in the home aquarium.

A pair of pearl gouramis (*Trichogaster leerii*). Members of this species are often timid; therefore, it is important that they be disturbed as rarely as possible, especially during spawning.

"As soon as the young Macropodus start feeding on Artemia larvae, they are over the worst. From that point on their growth is quite rapid..."

Aquarium Inhabitants

Hygrophila polysperma .

"Repeated trimming of [Hygrophila polysperma] plant stimulates lateral shoots, giving the plant a bushy appearance."

I have already discussed some details about various plant and fish species in our aquarium, but in many instances I could do little more than just give the name. Here now is further information about the inhabitants of our aquarium.

WATER PLANTS
Hygrophila polysperma
Habitat: India to Malay

Water wisteria looks best when planted in bunches.

Peninsula. Family Acanthaceae. In its native habitat this plant tends to grow above water. Undemanding and suitable for all tank sizes. Easily reproduced through shoots. Repeated trimming of plant stimulates lateral shoots, giving the plant a bushy appearance. Does require sufficient light for proper development. Most effective in bunches.

Water Wisteria
Hygrophila difformis
Habitat: Southeast Asia. Sometimes described as water fern. With decorative, deeply forked leaves. Hardy, rapidly growing plant, ideally suited for preliminary planting. Should not be crowded, keep about 7 cm apart. Reproduces easily from shoots; these can be cut off and planted directly into the substrate. Root development is rapid. Most suitable for peripheral and background planting.

Ludwigia
These plants have a worldwide distribution. A hybrid *Ludwigia*, a cross between *L. palustris* and *L. repens*, is the most common

aquarium *Ludwigia.* A hardy plant which can be highly recommended provided tank temperatures do not exceed 25°C (77°F). Will grow above the water surface. Must be trimmed at regular intervals by removing shoots. Can be planted in relatively dense, bush-like groups.

Amazon Swordplant
Echinodorus parviflorus

Undemanding but decorative low-growing plant from the Upper Ucayali River, Peru. Tends to grow primarily above the water surface in its native range for most of the year. Juvenile plants are also suitable for smaller aquariums. If given enough room (larger tanks) and ample light it will develop into a very large plant with dark leaves. Eventually a flower stalk develops. However, underwater specimens do not produce a flower, but instead these develop directly into juvenile plants. They already have roots and thus can be pushed into the substrate (the stalk may have to be weighted down with a rock). They

must not however be separated from the mother plant for at least another month, if at all.

"If given enough room. . .and ample light it [Echinodorus parviflorus] will develop into a very large plant with dark leaves."

Ludwigia repens. *Ludwigia* species are bog plants.

The Amazon swordplant (*Echinodorus parviflorus*) reproduces by runners which float upward from the substrate.

Cryptocoryne affinis

Habitat: Dark jungle streams on Malay Peninsula. Very undemanding; will grow under very unfavorable lighting conditions. Once it has been planted in a home aquarium, it should be left undisturbed as much as possible. Develops many substrate runners. Leaves have a knobby, corrugated texture, usually dark reddish-brown underneath. Well-suited for plant groups in the middle ground of the aquarium, as well as along the sides. One of the most common and hardiest of the *Cryptocoryne* species.

"Very undemanding [Cryptocoryne affinis]: will grow under very unfavorable lighting conditions."

Cryptocoryne affinis. Cryptocorynes can survive in relatively weak aquarium light.

Java Fern
Microsorium pteropus

This plant belongs to the particularly hardy plants which can get by on relatively low light levels. Best kept as an "epiphyte" on roots and rocks. To assure proper attachment the plants must initially be fastened with a rubber band until the roots have taken hold in the substrate. Reproduction is by means of daughter plants, which will soon develop all over the roots and leaves of the mother plant. The aquarist must be patient with transplanting the juvenile plants. Strangely enough, Java ferns grow better the more they are kept close together. The robust leaves of the Java fern are not attacked by even the most persistent plant (herbivorous) feeders.

Swamp corkscrew (*Vallisneria spiralis*).

"Because of its rapid growth, water sprite has to be frequently exchanged for a smaller specimen. Even in large tanks it will soon become too large and occupy too much space."

Hygrophila corymbosa.

Water Sprite
Ceratopteris thalicroides

Widely distributed throughout the tropics. This is considered to be a particularly fast growing plant under aquarium conditions. Can be kept as either a floating plant or as a bottom plant. Must not be pushed into the substrate. Instead, the root should be weighted down with a rock and the roots will grow on their own. Because of its rapid growth, water sprite has to be frequently exchanged for a smaller specimen. Even in very large tanks it will soon become too large and occupy too much space. Especially when kept as a floating plant, the mother plant must be replaced with some of the small daughter plants. Otherwise the tank surface will become grown over rather quickly, thus cutting out the light for the plants below.

Hygrophila corymbosa

Habitat: Southeast Asia. This solid stemmed plant is among the most rapidly growing of aquarium plants. Therefore it is ideally suited for use during the initial planting phase. It will

quickly grow above the water surface, and with adequate illumination it will produce violet-blue flowers. Reproduction is particularly easy by means of cuttings planted in the substrate, where they quickly develop roots. Unfortunately, however, adult plants which have been trimmed repeatedly become unsightly. They should be replaced with fresh cuttings. This plant is ideally suited for the background of the aquarium or along its sides.

Hygrophila stricta

This species is very reminiscent of *H. corymbosa* but with narrower leaves, which are set in closer sequence. It is a very

decorative stemmed plant which is suitable for peripheral planting. Also serves as a solitary centerpiece plant. Reproduction is by means of cuttings from a mother plant.

Swamp Corkscrew
Vallisneria spiralis
   The swamp corkscrew is ideally suited for start-up planting. It is undemanding, grows rapidly and one can virtually watch new substrate runners shooting out. From the sparse start-up planting there will soon be a virtual *Vallisneria* forest. With this plant it is particularly important that it is not planted too deeply in the substrate. The runners do not have to be cut off from the adult

"It [Hygrophila stricta] is a very decorative plant which is suitable for peripheral planting. Also serves as a solitary centerpiece plant."

Corkscrew Vallisneria (*Vallisneria asiatica biwaensis*).

The true Amazon swordplant (*Echinodorus amazonicus*).

"This plant [Vallisneria spiralis] is ideally suited for being planted in groups in the back or along the sides of an aquarium."

plant. The ribbon-like long leaves will soon reach the water surface and will continue to grow, drifting along the surface. If the leaves start to keep too much light away from the plants below, they can be cut back with a pair of scissors. It will not damage the plants but it tends to slow down their growth slightly. This plant is ideally suited for being planted in groups in the

Cryptocoryne wendtii.

back or along the sides of an aquarium.

This plant has derived its name—swamp corkscrew—from the very long flower stalks which grow up to the surface in a strongly spiraled manner. After the flowers have been fertilized they grow spirally downwards again towards deeper water layers.

Corkscrew Vallisneria
Vallisneria asiatica biwaensis

A very decorative bottom plant from Southeast Asia with long narrow leaves which are twisted like a corkscrew. There are, however, plants with straight leaves. They are distinguished from the swamp corkscrew by the presence of a finely serrated leaf margin. Apart from that it should be kept just like the swamp corkscrew. Since it grows less rapidly, cutting back is not advisable.

True Amazon Swordplant
Echinodorus amazonicus

A bottom-growing plant from the Amazon Basin. It is often also described as the narrow-leaved Amazon swordplant. It is a very impressive solitary centerpiece plant which requires quite a bit of space. When given enough light it produces runners.

"A very decorative bottom plant [Vallisneria asiatica biwaensis] from Southeast Asia with long narrow leaves which are twisted like a corkscrew."

The red tiger lotus (*Nymphaea lotus*).

Top right: **Horned water sprite (*Ceratopteris cornuta*).** *Bottom right:* **Rotala (*Rotala macrantha*).** *Left:* **Water milfoil (*Myriophyllum brasiliense*).**

Red Tiger Lotus
Nymphaea lotus

Because of its intensely reddish-brown leaf color and large, round leaves, this is one of the most conspicuous aquarium plants. Therefore, it is particularly well suited as an eye-catching centerpiece plant. It thrives best in soft water which is not too warm, but it can also be kept in medium hard water. It responds well to carbon dioxide supplement and iron fertilizer. Prefers a substrate which has been slightly enriched with clay (do not wash the lowest substrate layer!!) and it needs a lot of light. Sensitive to transplanting. Has to be planted very shallowly into the substrate.

A closely related species, the green tiger lotus, is also very decorative. It has large, light

green leaves with an irregular pattern of brown spots.

Cryptocoryne wendtii

Habitat: Sri Lanka. It occurs in several different varieties. It is

Right: Water milfoil (*Myriophyllum hippuriodes*). *Left:* Cabomba (*Cabomba australis*). *Bottom:* Red Cabomba growing wild in Brazil.

"A closely related species, the green tiger lotus, is also very decorative. It has large, light green leaves with an irregular pattern of brown spots."

Cabomba (Cabomba caroliniana).

"The numerous species in the genus Myriophyllum are all stemmed plants which are characterized by the presence of a multitude of tiny hair-like leaves."

Barclaya longifolia.

undemanding in respect to water condition, light availability and substrate. Reproduction is the same as for *C. affinis*, in the form of runners. It is ideally suited for plant groups in the middle region of the aquarium.

Horned Water Sprite
Ceratopteris cornuta

This plant occurs mainly in tropical Africa. It is closely related to the common water sprite and should be kept under similar conditions. Water sprite can be cultivated either as a floating plant or planted in the substrate. Distinguishing these two species is not always easy, but the leaves of *C. cornuta* are usually more roundish and less forked. Reproduction is adventitious by means of plants which form along the leaf margins in adult plants.

Water Milfoils
Myriophyllum

The numerous species in the genus *Myriophyllum* are all stemmed plants which are characterized by the presence of a multitude of tiny hair-like leaves. Determining a particular species is usually not easy. Maintenance of some *Myriophyllum* species is often difficult; their delicate leaves tend to collect silt. There are some very decorative varieties with reddish leaves. Unfortunately, they tend to lose this coloration quickly under aquarium conditions unless they are given a lot of light. *Myriophyllum* species must not be kept too warm!

Rotala macrantha

A difficult but very attractive plant which needs a well-established tank with soft water, excellent carbon dioxide conditions, occasionally some iron supplements and especially a lot of light. If these conditions are provided, this stemmed plant develops magnificently colored wine red leaves.

Cabomba

The members of this genus, with their densely spaced, delicate leaves, are among the most attractive stemmed plants for the aquarium. Regrettably, they are also rather difficult to keep and will only last in an aquarium if optimum conditions are provided. The basic requirements are soft, slightly acid water, ideal carbon dioxide conditions and, especially, a lot of light.

"The members of this genus [Cabomba], with their densely spaced, delicate leaves, are among the most attractive stemmed plants for the aquarium."

Cryptocoryne willisii, also known as Cryptocoryne axelrodi.

Sagittaria subulata pusilla.

Barclaya
Barclaya longifolia

This tropical water lily from Thailand is very decorative but is also a slow grower. It is not too uncommon to have this attractive solitary plant flower in an aquarium. Should this happen and the 1 to 2 mm seeds have been collected, young plants can be raised in a shallow water bowl or other container. But this plant needs a lot of light, temperatures of at least 24°C (75°F) and some clay in the substrate. Growth phases are often intermittent and the plant must not be disturbed when growth has temporarily stopped. Unfortunately, snails like to feed on this plant!

Sagittaria subulata pusilla

In growth form and type this plant is strongly reminiscent of a dwarf *Vallisneria*. It also reproduces by means of substrate runners. A hardy, carpet-forming plant, ideally suited for the foreground of an aquarium.

Cryptocoryne willisii

Formerly often known as *C. axelrodi*. It is a small species with elongated, green, somewhat stiff leaves. An undemanding plant which is ideally suited for foreground planting. A slow grower, it can take years for a small colony to develop into a real *Cryptocoryne* lawn. A group of about ten plants often does better when individual plants are placed separately in the substrate. As with all *Cryptocoryne* species, this one must be moved as little as possible because any new growth places a lot of stress on the plant. Will grow distinctly faster when the light level is increased.

Dwarf Amazon Swordplant
Echinodorus tenellus

This is the smallest *Echinodorus* species. It has grass-like, narrow leaves which tend to form regular underwater carpets. It should be placed in the foreground of an aquarium. Needs sufficient light and carbon dioxide for proper growth. Two other dwarf Amazon swordplant species (*E. bolivianus* and *E. quadricostatus xinguensis*) which are closely related to *E. tenellus* also tend to form attractive underwater carpets. They too require more light, and they are known to respond favorably to iron supplements.

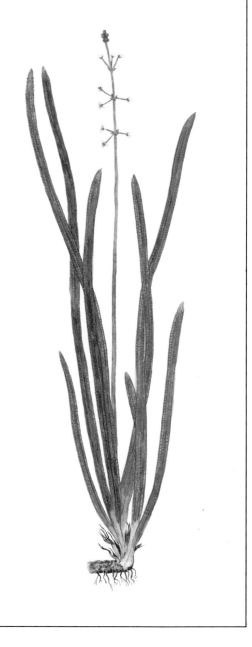

Dwarf Amazon swordplant (*Echinodorus quadricostatus*).

Dwarf Amazon swordplant (*Echinodorus tenellus*).

A long-finned zebra danio (*Brachydanio rerio*).

AQUARIUM FISHES
Zebra Danio
Brachydanio rerio

This striped fish comes from the eastern section of the Indian subcontinent and from Bangladesh. Hardly any other schooling fish is as active and still as peaceful as this one. They are almost constantly on the move, often chasing each other in harmless play. It is a typical schooling fish, and therefore a minimum of six is a must if this species is kept. Zebra danios do not place any significant demands on the water quality or food. The sexes can only be distinguished by the more slender build of the male. A breeding pair scatters its eggs in the aquarium usually during the early morning hours. While zebra danios spawn readily in a community tank, young are not likely to be reared in such a tank as the eggs are usually eaten.

Head and Tail Light Tetra
Hemigrammus ocellifer

A very quiet schooling fish which belongs to the tetras. Most tetras have a small adipose fin a short distance behind the actual dorsal fin; the head and tail light is no exception. Moreover, this is in every respect an undemanding fish, but it must be kept in a school and never alone. The native range is the Amazon Basin and Guyana. It is indeed a delightful fish with its slightly abrupt, almost jerking swimming movements and the lantern-like iridescent spots in the upper iris and in front of the dark spot at the base of the tail. A school of these fish kept in a darkish aquarium is most effective, as that is the sort of environment they like best. Therefore, it is recommended to keep a partial cover of *Ceratopteris* on the surface of the tank.

Platy
Xiphophorus maculatus

This is another type of fish which likes to be kept together with some more of its own kind, but they are not typical schooling fish, such as zebra danios and head and tail lights. Platies originally came from Central America. They are livebearers of the family Poeciliidae, related to

Left: Head and tail light tetras (*Hemigrammus ocellifer*). *Bottom left:* Black tetras (*Gymnocorymbus ternetzi*). *Bottom right:* A school of cardinal tetras (*Paracheirodon axelrodi*).

the killifishes. Platies are active, very peaceful fish. They occur in a wide variety of color strains, including some which are bright red and some which are red with black fins (red wagtail platies). Males can be recognized by their movable, rod-shaped copulating organ modified from the anal fin. In juveniles and females the anal fin is fan-shaped. Females which have been fertilized by a male will give birth to fully developed live young. In order to avoid being eaten by the other tank inhabitants, they immediately have to flee into plant thickets. Even their own parents cannot distinguish them from their regular food. When young platies are seen in a community tank, attempt to catch them and place

"Platies are active, peaceful fish. They occur in a wide variety of color strains, including some of which are bright red and some of which are red with black fins (red wagtail platies)."

Red platies (*Xiphophorus maculatus*).

Aphyosemion georgiae . This species is not recommended for beginners— it requires soft acidic water, especially for breeding.

Blue platies. Some platy varieties were developed through hybridization with swordtails.

Blue notho (*Nothobranchius jubbi*). Like most killifishes, this species is not recommended for the community tank.

The gold-cheek krib (*Pelvicachromis subocellatus*) is a peaceful krib that is becoming more and more common in home aquaria.

Kribensis (*Pelvicachromis pulcher*).

"The kribensis . . . comes from the coastal waters of West Africa. Make every attempt to get a pair."

them into a small separate tank (a large jar will do). These young will start to feed immediately on finely ground dried fish foods.

Kribensis
Pelvicachromis pulcher

This fish is not as peaceful as those fish described so far. But on the other hand it is especially interesting and a caring and dedicated "fish parent." Therefore, we should not miss an opportunity to observe the breeding behavior of these unusual fish.

The kribensis (also called "Krib") comes from the coastal waters of West Africa. Make every attempt to get a pair. The female can be recognized by the presence of one or two dark spots with a light margin on the posterior part of the dorsal fin. In males, however, these spots are absent and instead they are

An albino krib.

A pair of kribs (*Pelvicachromis pulcher*).

"This fish [P. pulcher] is a cave brooder. Therefore, it requires some simulated rocky caves in the aquarium."

sometimes present on the upper part of the tail. Usually the females are slightly more colorful, with a more compact body than males, and their fins are less drawn out.

This fish is a cave brooder. Therefore, it requires some simulated rocky caves in the aquarium. Alternatively, we can also use one half of a coconut shell placed in such a position that a small entrance hole remains open. If we are lucky we can watch the pair spawning by shining a flashlight into the cave.

Once we see that the pair is cleaning the cave and carrying sand out of the cave, spawning is not far off. By then the female's abdomen will have swollen; and finally a short spawning tube protrudes from the anal opening. Each pair will lay about 200 to 300 eggs, which they usually attach to the roof of the cave.

Once spawning has been completed the female will

Kribensis. Members of this species are cave brooders.

After spawning, kribensis parents take turns mouthing the eggs and circulating water over the eggs by fanning them.

Hatching takes place in one or two days; four or five days later the fry have absorbed their yolk sacs and therefore begin to search for food.

Kribensis (*Pelvicachromis pulcher*) color variety from the Kenema region.

"Once spawning has been completed the female will usually remain in the cave or very close by for the next few days. The male then tries to keep all other fish away from the proximity of the cave."

usually remain in the cave or very close by for the next few days. The male then defends the territory and tries to keep all other fish away from the proximity of the cave. Normally the other tank inhabitants will not be seriously hurt by the male's attacks. In very small tanks or with females which are particularly aggressive, the female can make the life of her mate very difficult. Therefore it is important to watch the fish closely and if need be to take the male out of the tank. Otherwise he can get killed by the female!

A few days later the female emerges from the cave with an entire swarm of young. Then we have real problems—do we want to raise the young? Either the parents will defend their brood extremely vigorously (then we

Kribensis color form from the Kasewe region.

A female kribensis laying eggs inside her cave.

"Either the parents will defend their brood extremely vigorously (then we have to worry about the other fish in the tank) or the other fish will eat the young cichlids one by one, and a few days later the entire school of young cichlids will have vanished."

have to worry about the other fish in the tank) or the other fish will eat the young cichlids one by one, and a few days later the entire school of young cichlids will have vanished. In a community tank the latter usually happens, but at least we have made some fascinating observations.

If we want to breed this fish anyway, we have several options.

We can remove all other tank inhabitants and keep only the pair and its young in the tank. Alternatively, we siphon the young out of the tank with a hose and transfer them to a special rearing tank. Initially we have to feed newly hatched brine shrimp larvae to the young cichlids.

An adult kribensis along with young fry.

Like the various kribensis species, the three species shown below and on the facing page come from Africa, but they are much more aggressive than the kribs.

Hornet tilapia (*Tilapia bettikoferi*). Members of this species have been known to torment other fishes and decimate aquarium plants; therefore, they are not good community members.

Opposite: A pair of Burton's mouthbrooders (Haplochromis burtoni). This species is hardy and easy to breed but should only be kept with other big tough fishes.

A pair of julies (*Julidochromis ornatus*). In the aquarium, this krib relative is a very picky eater.

Siamese flying fox (*E. siamensis*). In Thailand, this species is known as the lady's fingernail fish.

A pair of Siamese flying foxes.

Siamese Flying Fox
Epalzeorhynchus siamensis

Habitat: Southeast Asia. This fish is quite rightly considered to be an algae eater, so this is a very useful fish for the aquarium, especially since it will not attack water plants. Generally speaking, this is a peaceful fish, although they occasionally tend occasionally to chase each other. It requires a fair amount of heat, so the temperature must not be permitted to fall below 24°C (75°F). *E. siamensis* has not yet been bred in captivity.

Siamese flying fox.

"This fish [E. siamensis] is quite rightly considered to be an algae eater, so this is a very useful fish for the aquarium, especially since it will not attack water plants."

Flying fox (*E. kalopteris*), a close relative of the Siamese flying fox.

"This delicate little fish [Capoeta titteya] comes from the shaded streams of Sri Lanka."

The red-striped barb (*Puntius bimaculatus*) is an active schooling fish that has been known to be a fin-nipper.

Cherry Barb
Capoeta titteya

This delicate little fish comes from the shaded streams of Sri Lanka. Males are sometimes a bit aggressive towards each other and schooling behavior is not as defined as, for instance, in zebra danios. Nevertheless, the small "arguments" among these fish are generally harmless, and indeed they tend to make them more interesting. Sometimes they withdraw into plant thickets in order to rest.

During the spawning season females have a fuller body shape and have a deep cherry red coloration. Breeding cherry barbs in a community tank should not be considered.

Half-striped barb (*Capoeta semifasciolatus*). This species is not as common in home aquaria as the cherry barb.

A pair of spawning cherry barbs (Capoeta titteya).

Tiger barb
(*Capoeta
tetrazona*).

Capoeta pentazona, the five-barred barb.

A pair of neon tetras (*Paracheirodon innesi*).

False bleeding heart tetra

Flame Tetra
Hyphessobrycon flammeus

A particularly peaceful fish and without doubt the most undemanding of all tetras. It comes from the vicinity of Rio de Janeiro. Individually it is not a very spectacular fish, but it is very attractive in a school, particularly in a tank with floating plant cover.

The most easily bred tetra species, its young are virtually impossible to raise in a community tank because of predation by the other fish. Males can be distinguished from the fuller-bodied females by their black-bordered anal fin.

Flame tetras (*H. flammeus*). These are outgoing, convivial fish.

"The most easily bred tetra species, its [H. flammeus] young are virtually impossible to raise in a community tank because of predation by other fish."

A pair of flame tetras. Members of this species are relatively easy to breed.

Flame tetras (*H. flammeus*) look great in a large, well-planted aquarium.

A trio of callistus tetras (*H. callistus*).

A trio of cardinal tetras (*Paracheirodon axelrodi*).

Chinese Algae Eater
Gyrinocheilus aymonieri

A hardy, undemanding algae-eating fish from Southeast Asia which can attain considerable longevity in an aquarium. In its native habitat this fish lives in rapidly flowing waters. As an adaptation to this lifestyle the mouth of this fish has become modified into a suction disc. Older specimens sometimes "harass" other fish with their cleaning behavior. Nevertheless, it is a peaceful and highly recommended species which so far has not been bred in captivity.

Chinese algae eater (*Gyrinocheilus aymonieri*). This fish is a strict vegetarian that does a wonderful job of cleaning up the tank.

Chinese algae eater. This species, like many, is usually much smaller in captivity than in the wild.

Chinese algae eater cleaning up a leaf.

Chinese algae eater cleaning up a root.

Corydoras paleatus

This is one of a number of very hardy, undemanding catfish species from South America. In smaller or larger groups they tend to scour through the sand along the bottom in search of food. There must be at least some open sand patches in the aquarium; sharp-edged gravel may cause injuries to the very sensitive barbels of these fish.

At feeding times it is important to make sure that these fish—at the bottom of the aquarium—actually get enough food. This is best done by giving an extra portion just for the catfish at night immediately after the light has been turned off. In contrast to most other fish, they can still find their food in the dark because they rely on their senses of taste and touch and not on their sight.

Corydoras paleatus is sometimes called the peppered cory.

A pair of
*Corydoras
paleatus* catfish.
This species has
the distinction
of having been
discovered by
Charles Darwin.

A blue
*Corydoras
paleatus* catfish.

A pair of three-lined catfish (*Corydoras trilineatus*).

Corydoras aeneus

A catfish with a metallic green sheen. Everything that has been said about *C. paleatus* also applies to this species. It too comes from sandy shallow water zones in South American jungle streams.

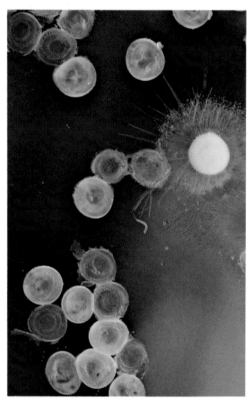

Top: Aeneus catfish (*Corydorus aeneus*). *Center:* Aeneus catfish eggs which have become fungused.

A pair of prize-winning aeneus catfish.

An albino
aeneus catfish.

Aeneus catfish.
Both *Corydoras
aeneus* and
*Corydoras
paleatus* prefer
to breed in a
colony of two
males to one
female.

Burgess's catfish (*Corydoras burgessi*).

Tail-spot catfish (*Corydoras caudimaculatus*).

A pair of wavy
catfish
(*Corydoras
undulatus*).

Blue catfish
(*Corydoras
nattereri*).

A pair of McCulloch's rainbowfish (*Melanotaenia maccullochii*). This photo was taken in Cairns, Australia, part of their native range.

McCulloch's rainbowfish. To achieve maximum coloration, rainbowfish should receive an hour or two of direct sunlight each day.

McCulloch's Rainbowfish
Melanotaenia maccullochii

Here we have an active and at the same time very peaceful schooling fish from northeastern Australia. It is durable, but should be kept in medium hard to hard water.

Breeding this fish is easy because the eggs are rather hardy and the newly hatched young are not eaten by their parents. However, in a community tank it is difficult to rear young rainbowfish because the other tank inhabitants will usually feed on them. Yet, if we are very observant we may be able to detect the crystal clear transparent eggs which hang from plants suspended by tiny threads. If we carefully remove them and transfer them into a separate container we may be able to breed this species even when the parents are in a community tank.

A pair of McCulloch's rainbowfish. During the spawning season, the color of the male rainbowfish intensifies.

"*Breeding this fish [*Melanotaenia maccullochii*] is easy because the eggs are rather hardy and the newly hatched young are not eaten by their parents.*"

An attractive color morph of McCulloch's rainbowfish.

Black molly

A pair of gold dust mollies. Note the difference in the coloration of these two fish.

There has been much hybridization among the molly species; this fish is a male *Poecilia latipinna.*

"Black mollies are livebearers ... The black coloration often develops only gradually with increasing age of the fish."

A striking black molly.

Black Molly
Poecilia species (hybrid)

This impressive-looking jet-black fish has been developed from a gray-colored wild form through the process of selective breeding. Other varieties developed in captivity include forms which have extended upper and lower caudal fin rays (lyretail mollies).

Black mollies are livebearers. For sex determination and breeding refer to the platy. The black coloration often develops only gradually with increasing age of the fish.

Black mollies like tanks with harder water and higher temperature; they should never be kept below 25°C (77°F). They are also useful as algae eaters. Apart from regular dried foods, they must also be given specific foods prepared from plant materials.

A black molly and a silver molly.

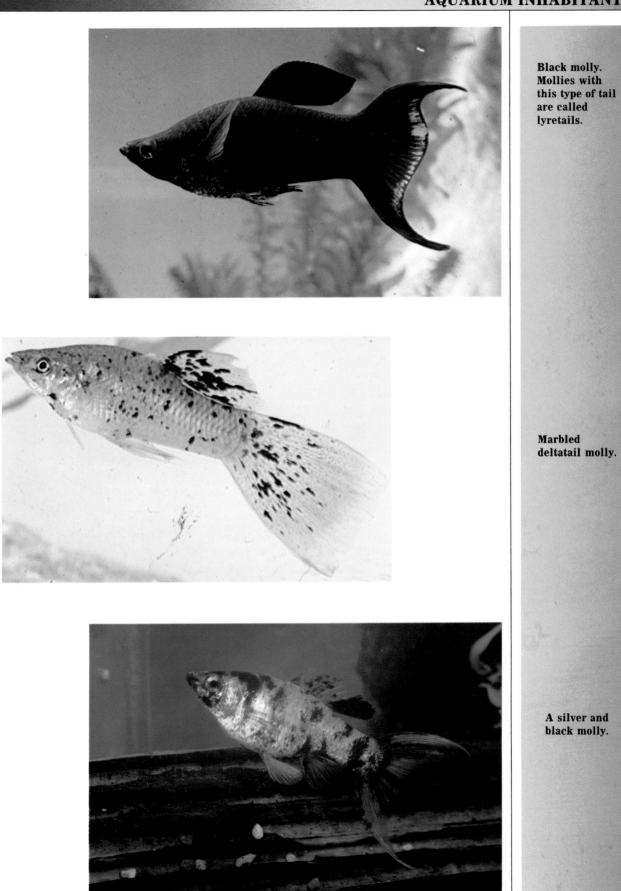

Black molly. Mollies with this type of tail are called lyretails.

Marbled deltatail molly.

A silver and black molly.

A truly "red" red rainbowfish (*Glossolepis incisus*).

"Adult males have a magnificent orange-red color; the somewhat smaller females are brass-colored."

A breeding pair of red rainbowfish. Some experts believe that for successful spawning, several males should be kept with one female.

Red Rainbowfish
Glossolepis incisus

A very attractive schooling fish which requires larger tanks. The maximum size of this species is 15 cm, but it takes some time until this size is reached. Even at that size they are still peaceful towards the other tank inhabitants. Adult males have a magnificent orange-red color; the somewhat smaller females are brass-colored.

Red rainbowfish.

A red rainbowfish (*Glossolepis incisus*).

Red rainbowfish. This species has become very popular in recent years, especially among West German aquarists.

A pair of red rainbowfish. Members of this species inhabit lake regions in New Guinea.

A pair of red rainbowfish.

A male Madagascar rainbowfish (*Bedotia geayi*).

A trio of Madagascar rainbowfish.

Madagascar Rainbowfish
Bedotia geayi

Habitat: Madagascar. This fish must be given medium hard to hard water which is on the alkaline side. In fact, that is the type of water in most municipal water supply systems. This fish is a peaceful schooling fish which has essentially the same care and breeding requirements as listed for other rainbowfish. In some strains the characteristic red in the tail fin is absent.

Swordtail
Xiphophorus helleri

Swordtails are live-bearers from Mexico. They are strongly reminiscent of platies, and indeed both are closely related to each other. The males are characterized by the presence of a sword-like extension of the tail and they exhibit an impressive courtship behavior. There are not too many fish which are able to swim as fast backward as swordtail males.

"Swordtails are live-bearers from Mexico. They are strongly reminiscent of platies, and indeed both are closely related to each other."

A pair of swordtails (*Xiphophorus helleri*), male and female. The male is the fish with the sword.

Similar to black mollies, there are also a number of special strains which have been produced through selective breeding. Yet, the greenish original form is particularly active and highly recommended for a community tank. The required temperature range is 22 to maximally 25°C (72 to 77°F). The red forms prefer temperatures around 25°C (77°F).

It is quite possible to produce hybrids from crossings between swordtails and platies. In fact, some commercially available forms have been derived this way. Sexual differences and reproduction are the same as given for the platy. While it is difficult to save any young born in a community tank, some may survive if the tank has ample plant cover and if the fry are noticed and removed in time to be reared separately.

A pair of high-fin swordtails. This variety was perfected by selectively breeding swordtails that had high dorsal fins.

"It is quite possible to produce hybrids from crossings between swordtails and platies. In fact, some commercially available forms have been derived this way."

A piebald swordtail produced in Sri Lanka.

Left: A female
pineapple
twinbar
swordtail
(*Xiphophorus
helleri*). *Right:*
A gold flame
twinbar
swordtail.
Bottom: A pair
of swordtails.

Swordtail. Several swordtail varieties have been produced through hybridization with other *Xiphophorus* species.

Male gold flame twinbar swordtail.

Opposite: Spike-tail paradise fish (*Macropodus cupanus*). *Top:* A pair of albino paradise fish (*Macropodus opercularis*). *Bottom:* Paradise fish.

Paradise Fish
Macropodus opercularis

Habitat: Eastern Asia, from Korea to southern Vietnam. This species lives in rice paddies and other standing, swampy waters. It is an attractive yet hardy fish which is quite suitable even for larger tanks with other species which are similarly undemanding. Adult males can be recognized by the extended tips of their dorsal, anal and tail fins. Females are less brightly colored and lack the extended fins. There are no particular requirements in respect to water quality and food. Water currents (from filters, circulating pumps, etc.) should be avoided as much as possible. This species prefers to have floating plants on the tank surface.

The pet shop trade offers black, blue, yellow and white color strains of this species. Very similar in care and breeding requirements are the Chinese paradise fish *(Macropodus chinensis)* and black paradise fish *(Macropodus concolor)*.

"The pet shop trade offers black, blue, yellow and white color strains of this species."

Siamese Fighting Fish
Betta splendens

The fighting fish, or more correctly the "Siamese fighting fish," is offered almost exclusively in the veiltail variety. Only males have these ornamental fins. In Thailand, male fighting fish are placed together in the same container to observe their fighting, and bets are placed in respect to the outcome of such fights. The fish used for that purpose are specially bred for their aggressive traits. Our fighting fish are far more peaceful and can easily be kept together with *other* peaceful species. But it is important not to keep more than one male in a community tank.

There are no special requirements in regard to water conditions and food; however, water currents must be kept to a minimum or—better yet—be completely absent. The temperature should not drop below 25°C (77°F) for any length of time.

The male builds a bubble nest at the surface and cares for the brood.

Siamese fighting fish occur in all sorts of colors. There are also some species of *Betta* which are mouthbrooders, where the male actually broods his progeny in a throat (gular) pouch. But these species are for specialists, and moreover they are rarely ever available through pet shops.

"The fighting fish, or more correctly the 'Siamese fighting fish,' is offered almost exclusively in the veiltail variety. Only males have these ornamental fins."

Opposite: Siamese fighting fish (Betta splendens).

Bright blue and red Siamese fighting fish.

137

Top: The Brunei beauty (*Betta macrostoma*) is a mouthbrooding betta. *Bottom:* A pair of Edith's bettas (*Betta edithae*).

Red fighting fish (*Betta coccina*). This "fighting fish" is small and rather shy when compared to some of its more boisterous relatives.

Banded betta (*Betta fasciata*).

Suggested Reading

**DR. AXELROD'S ATLAS OF
FRESHWATER AQUARIUM
FISHES**
**By Dr. Herbert R. Axelrod and
others**
ISBN 0-86622-748-2
TFH H-1077

Here is a truly beautiful and
immensely colorful book that
satisfies the long-existing need
for a comprehensive
identification guide to all
aquarium fishes that find their
way onto world markets. This
book describes and presents in
full-color photography not only
the popular aquarium fishes but
also the oddballs and weirdos of
the hobby; not just the
warmwater species but the
coldwater species as well; not
just the foreign fishes but the
domestics, too. But not all of this
text/photo-packed volume is
concerned with identification
and maintenance alone. In
addition to showing the fishes
and telling exactly what they are,
this book also provides practical
information—plus step-by-step
full-color photographic
sequences—about the spawning
of a number of species from
different families.

AQUARIUM PLANTS
By Dr. K. Rataj and T. Horeman
ISBN 0-87666-455-9
TFH H-966

Designed for use by aquarium
hobbyists, horticulturists,
botanists, and students, this
massive and highly colorful book
is the most complete volume ever
published about aquarium
plants. Written on a high school
level, *Aquarium Plants* includes
information on the cultivation of
aquatic plants, algae in the
aquarium, and reproduction in
aquatic plants—just some of the
many invaluable chapters
included in this book.

HANDBOOK OF FISH DISEASES
By Dieter Untergasser
ISBN 0-86622-703-2
TFH TS-123

This volume is by any yardstick
the finest, most useful book about
fish diseases ever offered to
aquarium hobbyists. Colorful,
comprehensive, and completely
understandable, *Handbook of Fish
Diseases* is loaded with necessary
information and good advice that
will save hobbyists' money and
fishes' lives wherever it is put to
use. Because of its simple style,
this magnificent volume makes
the diagnosis and treatment of
fish diseases easier and surer
than ever before. Keys to
recognizing diseases and
providing proper treatment are
presented in easy-to-follow
charts accompanied by excellent

full-color photographs, all taken by the author and never before published in an English-language book. By noting the symptoms shown by a fish, readers can use the keys to isolate the cause of the disease through process of elimination and simply follow up with the right treatment—also listed, of course. Chapters on fish anatomy, viral and bacterial diseases, fungal and algal diseases, parasites, tumors, genetic abnormalities and much, much more are supplemented by sections dealing with valuable techniques such as staining and microscopy. This book also contains an extensive list of drugs for treating fish diseases and, where possible, sources from which they can be obtained.

LIVEBEARING AQUARIUM FISHES
By Manfred Brembach
ISBN 0-86622-101-8
TFH PS-832

In this useful book, author Manfred Brembach takes the reader by the hand and leads them through the fascinating hobby keeping livebearing fishes. Topics include breeding, nutrition, and behavior, to name just a few.

BETTAS: A COMPLETE INTRODUCTION
By Walter Maurus
ISBN 0-86622-254-4 (hardcover); 0-86622-288-X (softcover)
TFH CO-005 (hardcover); CO-005S (softcover)

An updated version of the most famous *Betta* book ever published, this volume is loaded with 107 great full-color photographs and five drawings of the fascinating Siamese fighting fish. Included are many different *Betta* species, not just the most common. Feeding, breeding, raising the fry, color and finnage varieties—this book has it all.

AN ATLAS OF FRESHWATER AND MARINE CATFISHES
By Dr. Warren E. Burgess
ISBN 0-86622-891-8
TFH H-1097

No book has ever attempted to deal with the catfishes (all 32 families) in their entirety—until now! Here at last is the definitive book on catfishes, dealing with the more than 2000 species. The text of this volume treats the catfishes family by family, giving for each the morphological characters as well as any biological information that may be available. A key to the genera contained within a particular family is offered whenever possible, and descriptions of each genus are provided along with an outline drawing of a species of almost every genus to help in generic recognition. Further discussions include biological information as well as spawning procedures for those species where they are known. At the end of each family write-up is a complete checklist of genera and species.

Index